Laptev Sea

East Siberian Sea

Central Siberian Plateau

Lena River

Siberia

Kolyma River

Kolyma

Arctic Circle

Lena River

Butugychag

Ust'-Omchug

Magadan

Bering Sea

Sea of Okhotsk

Lake Baikal

Amur River

Sakalin
Island

Pacific Ocean

© 2017 Jeffrey L. Ward

NEVER
REMEMBER

BY MASHA GESSEN AND
MISHA FRIEDMAN

SEARCHING FOR STALIN'S GULAGS
IN PUTIN'S RUSSIA

COLUMBIA GLOBAL REPORTS
NEW YORK

Never Remember
Searching for Stalin's Gulags in Putin's Russia
Copyright © 2018 by Masha Gessen and Misha Friedman
All rights reserved

Published by Columbia Global Reports
91 Claremont Avenue, Suite 515
New York, NY 10027
globalreports.columbia.edu
facebook.com/columbiaglobalreports
@columbiaGR

Never Remember: Searching for Stalin's Gulag's in Putin's Russia
has been made possible in part by a major grant from the
Wallenberg Executive Committee and the Weiser Center for
Emerging Democracies at the University of Michigan.

Library of Congress Control Number: 2016962829
ISBN: 9780997722963

Book design by Strick&Williams
Map design by Jeffrey L. Ward
Author photograph of Masha Gessen © Tanya Sazansky
Author photograph of Misha Friedman © Sergey Goroshko

Printed in China.

CONTENTS

PROLOGUE

Looking for Wallenberg

Of all the men who left and never returned, of all who were remembered and all who were forgotten, of all whose fate never let memory gain a foothold, none might have been sought as desperately or for as long as Raoul Wallenberg. Born in 1912 to a wealthy Swedish family, educated in the United States as an architect, Wallenberg found his calling, in 1944, in Nazi-occupied Hungary. As an envoy of neutral Sweden, Wallenberg used his position to create safe-houses for Jews, forge identity documents for Jews, and smuggle Jews out of the country to safety. Most Eastern European Jews had been murdered by then; the turn of the Hungarian Jews came last, when the world was generally aware of the Holocaust. Wallenberg was not the only foreign diplomat in Budapest racing to save Jews; he was not even the one ultimately credited with saving the greatest number of lives. He was the one who disappeared.

Wallenberg vanished after the Red Army entered Hungary. On January 17, 1945, he went to a meeting with Soviet officials and was never again seen by anyone who had known him. After the war Sweden worked to maintain neutrality in a divided Europe. An energetic search for the missing diplomat could have undermined these efforts. Wallenberg was written off.

A decade after Wallenberg's disappearance—a decade after the end of the Second World War—the Soviet Union released surviving German prisoners of war, and they brought memories of Wallenberg. They had heard of him—or heard him knocking on cell walls and floors, tapping out messages from solitary confinement in Moscow's Lefortovo Prison. Stalin was dead, the new Soviet government was presenting a friendlier face to the West, and Sweden began asking for an accounting. The United States, worried about the newly seductive Soviet posture, did what it could to arouse interest in Wallenberg among the Swedish media—as a public-opinion hedge against coziness with the USSR. Moscow finally produced a handwritten document indicating that Wallenberg had died of a heart attack in Soviet custody on July 17, 1947.

It was Alexander Solzhenitsyn who rekindled the search for Wallenberg nearly twenty years later. In Stockholm to collect his Nobel Prize for literature—four years after it was awarded in 1970, before he was exiled from the Soviet Union—the man who had memorialized the Gulag by putting a myriad voices on paper told Wallenberg's parents that their son could still be alive. Over the next fifteen years, the urgency of the search continued to intensify.

There were rumors. One had it that a character in *The Gulag Archipelago,* an apparition among inmates who wears his hair long and is transported in a separate compartment, who says that he is a Swede from a wealthy family named Anderson, was in fact Wallenberg. He was not. But he could have been. Anything was possible in the absence of knowledge. If Anderson had been Wallenberg, that would have meant that Wallenberg was still alive in the 1950s.

There were witnesses. They claimed that they had seen Wallenberg in a jail, in a camp, in a prison infirmary, in a mental hospital, in Moscow, in central Russia, in Siberia, in the Far East, in the 1950s, the 1970s, and even the 1980s. All of them were lying. Whether these liars were seeking attention, money, or nothing at all, their falsifications landed in fertile soil. Wallenberg's family longed to believe that he was alive, and the CIA kept tending to the story, to ensure that Sweden did not forget the Soviet crime against it.

Thirty-five years after his disappearance, Raoul Wallenberg began gathering international recognition. There were books, films,

monuments, streets, and squares, in New York City, Washington, and Stockholm. There were honorary citizenships: American, Canadian, and Israeli. The idea that the man being honored might still be alive—Wallenberg would have been in his seventies in the 1980s—gave this growing international movement its energy and an edge of desperation. The idea that he might have died in a Soviet prison camp during the decades of relative silence gave it an edge of shame. I first learned of Wallenberg from an article my mother wrote for a Russian-language emigre newspaper in New York. She wrote that Wallenberg was "a man who tried to save the world whom the world failed to save."

Perestroika began in 1985. The policy of glasnost—"openness"—started loosening information from KGB archives. Organizations that called themselves "Memorial Societies" began forming in cities and towns all over the USSR, for the purpose of excavating the memory of the Gulag. Soviet citizens started asking what had happened to members of their families, and getting some answers.

Wallenberg's siblings traveled to Moscow in October 1989 (his parents had died) and had an audience with a top secret-police official. "It turned out that the points of departure for the conversation diverged strongly," one of Wallenberg's biographers later wrote. "The siblings had come in order to free their brother. The KGB general had been assigned the task of once and for all convincing the family that Wallenberg was dead." Both sides failed.

By this time, the Soviet Union had released all of its political prisoners. Except Wallenberg, if he was still alive. If he was not, then now, after a decade in which the world had been honoring his memory, he was the most famous person to have died in the Gulag. The Soviets formed a joint commission with the Swedes to look for Wallenberg. As part of its work, Moscow Memorial Society researchers were given access to the archives of prisons and Gulag directorates. As they looked for Wallenberg, they learned to navigate the documents, matching inmate numbers with names, and reconstructing events, tracing transfer orders and interrogations summonses. "In the search for Wallenberg, we entered the kitchen of state terror," one of the Memorial researchers, Arseny Roginsky, said a quarter century later.

They did not find him. Roginsky and most of his colleagues concluded that he must indeed have died on July 17, 1947; all the sightings reported since had been fictions. But they never found all the documents that would have laid out his fate. They never saw his personal file, and they harbored doubts about the handwritten document presented in lieu of a death certificate back in 1957.

While the commission worked, the Soviet Union collapsed, Russia ventured into democracy and retreated from it, public interest in the history of state terror waned, and access to Gulag archives was once again restricted. Facing an ever more unpredictable present, Russians as a nation abandoned the project of uncovering the past. The information obtained by tens or hundreds of thousands of individuals looking for traces of their relatives never came together to form a picture of what had been done to Soviet society.

Between the early 1930s and the late 1950s tens of millions of Soviet citizens and thousands of foreigners were incarcerated in the hundreds of camps, prisons, and colonies that made up the Gulag. Millions died: Some were executed within days of arrest, some months or even years later, while hundreds of thousands were starved or effectively tortured to death. Several million more were subjected to deportations, the wholesale movement of

people that claimed hundreds of thousands more dead. The terror killed people who belonged to the Party and those who objected against it, those who were deemed unreliable because of their national or class provenance and those who transgressed against increasingly stringent rules. But most of all, it killed people without rhyme or reason. The Soviet killing machine was the biggest in a century of killing machines, and the most effective because it inspired fear in an entire population, which knew: no one was exempt. Not even a wealthy Swedish diplomat who had resisted the Nazis in occupied Budapest.

The Swedish-Russian commission finally presented its findings in a public event in Stockholm. The Russians, represented by officers of the FSB—the successor agency to the KGB—said that Wallenberg had died on July 17, 1947, but from a bullet rather than a heart attack. The Swedes said that the commission had been unable to establish conclusively that Wallenberg had died: He might still be alive. He would have been eighty-nine at the time of that press conference.

There was more. Interrogation summonses were discovered; in them, an inmate was identified by the number seven, and there was suspicion that Inmate Seven was Wallenberg. Inmate Seven was interrogated on July 23, 1947—six days after Wallenberg was supposed to have died. There was no indication that Inmate Seven had lived past July 23, 1947, but the search for Wallenberg had become the search for the truth about Wallenberg and now the official date of his death did not appear to be true. In 2015, a new group formed to "bring about a resolution of the case." It called itself the Raoul Wallenberg Research Initiative (RWI-70), where the "70" stood for the year of the seventieth anniversary of the end of the Second

World War, and of Wallenberg's disappearance. Wallenberg would have been one hundred and three.

The following spring I went to see Roginsky, one of the original Russian researchers in the case. Roginsky was still at Moscow Memorial Society, which was coming under increasingly vicious attacks from the Russian government. He was not much interested in talking about the case that had taught him to study the Gulag. "I am always getting inquiries from people who dream of proving that he was alive past July 17, 1947," he said. "But I am certain that he died, that he was probably killed. More could be learned, but for that we need full access to FSB archives." He thought that there probably existed a trail of correspondence between the Soviet foreign ministry and the secret police regarding Wallenberg—perhaps someday someone would find that. For now, and for the foreseeable future, there was only a slim folder of documents that all interested parties had seen, and of which most had received copies.

I had read that one set of copies was in the collection of the Jewish Museum in Moscow. The fact that this museum exists has been cited as one of the few incontrovertible examples of change in Russian society in the post-Soviet era. For most of its seventy-year history the Soviet state enforced antisemitism as a matter of policy more than of prejudice. But in the 2000s, with Jews well-represented among the Russian rich and powerful and among President Vladimir Putin's personal friends, the idea of a museum was born. Its full name is the Jewish Museum and Tolerance Center. It was an international effort: Russian Jewish funders, American academic consultants, and an American museum-design firm created it together. But first, the idea got the president's personal blessing—and then the FSB, in a gesture of goodwill, presented the museum

organizers with a set of copies of the Wallenberg documents. In 2008, when the gift was made, Russian media reported that the file would become a cornerstone of the future exhibit.

I had been to the museum a few times since it opened in 2012, but I could not recall how the Wallenberg documents were displayed. In the spring of 2016 I made a special trip to see just that. The museum occupies a vast hangarlike space, a 1920s Constructivist bus depot. Its exposition starts out telling a linear story, from the Jews of the Bible to the Jews of the Russian Empire, and then bifurcates at the Second World War. For the years 1941 to 1945, there are two story lines: the Holocaust and Jews serving in the Red Army. Both are breaks with Soviet historiography, which not only obscured the Holocaust but denied that there was anything particular about the Jewish experience of that war. This part of the museum culminates in a memorial space featuring millions of names culled from three databases: one from Yad Vashem, in Israel, which contains all known Jewish victims of the Holocaust; one from the Memorial Society, which contains those who died in battle during the Second World War; and one from the Russian defense ministry, which contains the names of acknowledged war heroes who died. Wallenberg has no place on any of those lists, or in any of these stories. This was not the kind of museum that took detours from its run through history in order to tell individual stories. Still, I looked. I examined every single display. I found nothing on Wallenberg.

I asked the staff and was redirected from one museum worker to another, until finally I found myself veritably pushed into a small room at the outer edge of the museum, behind the exposition. A woman sat working on something at the lone desk. The rest of the room was occupied by frames, displays, posters, and paintings. This

14 was a made-to-order museum, one that did not start out with a collection—so the architects foresaw no need for a warehousing space. Now everything that was not on display was here, in this room. The woman behind the desk looked and sounded alarmed.

"What are you doing here?"

The door closed behind me, and I stopped just beyond the threshold, in an attempt to lessen the shock from my intrusion.

"I am looking for the file on Raoul Wallenberg," I said, aware of how many times this phrase had been uttered elsewhere, by other people.

"Who are you?" asked the woman, the chief archivist of the museum.

"We are working on a book," I said. "Our interest is in memory. And forgetting."

Something changed just then. The woman relaxed and looked at me with something like curiosity.

"I am interested in memory, too," she said, as though it did not go without saying.

She told me that the culture of remembering had all but vanished. People kept coming, she said, bringing her artifacts that they thought of as rubbish. She said that they kept saying, "Take it or I'll toss it." They thought of their families' past as being full of junk, and they thought that junk was what museums collected. But this museum, built to house a single narrative multimedia exhibit, had no room for storage. The woman said that she had started running classes for children to teach them to be their families' memory keepers.

I had been allowed to approach the desk now. I showed her the news item that said that the museum had received the Wallenberg documents.

"We will look for him," she promised me. "Is he family of yours?" No.

I never heard back from the Jewish Museum and Tolerance Center.

There was a monument to Wallenberg in Moscow. I knew this, though I did not recall ever having seen it. Moscow is a city of many monuments—too many. The city had been the capital of not one but two empires—the Russian Empire, before Peter the Great moved the capital to St. Petersburg, and the Soviet one, after the Bolsheviks returned the seat of power to the Kremlin. Vladimir Lenin ascribed great importance to what he called "monumental propaganda," so the Bolsheviks quickly added their own layer of granite human forms to those of the czars. They also rearranged the monuments of the previous age, moving some out of sight, moving others to gaze in an ideologically correct direction. The city filled with monuments: It is in the nature of propaganda to try to be ubiquitous. Soviet heroes popped up in parks, playgrounds, and the courtyards of residential buildings. After Lenin died in 1924 and his mummified body was placed on display in a specially built mausoleum in Red Square, just outside the Kremlin, in the mental and emotional center of Russia, the whole country started decorating itself as the great Bolshevik's giant burial site. Citizens took up collections to erect Lenin monuments in front of their buildings and proceeded to place flowers at their plinths on all state holidays but especially on Lenin's birthday.

In August 1991, after a hard-line coup failed and when the Soviet regime teetered on the brink of collapse—the union would formally dissolve four months later—Muscovites celebrated by rearranging monuments again. A giant bronze likeness of Felix Dzershinsky, the founder of the Soviet secret police, was removed from its granite pedestal in front of the KGB headquarters in central Moscow. This was the monument that made the headlines—newspapers the world over erroneously reported that it was removed by a jubilant crowd, when in fact city authorities, terrified that the jubilant crowd would kill people by toppling the colossus, had sent a crane and removed the monument. Other Bolsheviks, including a few of the smaller Lenins, were also deposed that week. Also, a Stalin who had been hidden underground ever since he was posthumously denounced by Nikita Khrushchev thirty-five years earlier was dug up. These men of stone were warehoused on the large untended lawn in front of a newly constructed exhibit hall across from Gorky Park. Some had been damaged. Most had been defaced with paint, or decorated with graffiti. Some, like Dzerzhinsky, had been removed from their pedestals and so were simply laid on the ground (the pedestal remained, for a few years, in the square in front of secret-police headquarters topped with a wooden cross intended to symbolize the memory of victims of state terror). "In Russia monuments wander around cities in the dark, lose their shoes, fingers, hats, and heads," wrote memory scholar Svetlana Boym, my good friend and fellow emigre who focused on Russia in her work after the collapse of the USSR.

Open-air warehouses of a previous era's monuments are a fixture of post-imperial cities. The British historian David Cannadine has described visiting such a place on the outskirts of New Delhi: "a dozen immense statues, rising up from the bushes and the brambles, like the chessmen arrayed for that terrifying contest towards the end of the first Harry Potter film." These were emperors and viceroys originally placed by the British on the grand intersections of and at the ends of avenues in New Delhi "to be permanent monuments to men whose lives and deeds they deemed worthy of everlasting commemoration." The citizens of independent India did not, and they hauled them off to what Cannadine called "the final graveyard of the British empire."

Unlike the people of India, and unlike the citizens of newly independent states that had been part of the Soviet Union, Russians quickly abandoned their post-imperial project. In 1997 Svetlana and I went to see what had become of the monuments that had been placed on that untended lawn. Last either of us had checked, a few years earlier, they had been growing into the ground where they had been placed, haphazardly, and grass and small stray trees were growing taller all around them. Now, though, we discovered that the lawn had been mowed. Svetlana was delighted to find what had happened to the monuments themselves, which she described in her book *The Future of Nostalgia:*

Comrade Dzerzhinsky was standing tall again on his elaborate pedestal, cleaned up and retouched beneath glorious birch trees. The graffiti of August 1991 that ranged from "Freedom!" and "Down with the KGB!" to obscene words, punk and hippie slogans, and the anonymous inscription "To Felix from Misha," were all but gone. Grandpa Kalinin sat at a respectful distance under another tree, there being no trace of white circles under his eyes. Lenin and Brezhnev stood next to the faded neon sign "USSR is a stronghold of peace" made sometime in the 1980s, at the onset of the Afghan War, with a gigantic Soviet hammer and sickle to the left. Even Stalin, who until recently had been lying with his severed boot in front of him, was now standing upright in all his glory. The only part of his body that was missing was the nose. The Soviet politicians were surrounded by the greatest poets of all time—Lermontov, Esenin, Pushkin—as well as many foreign dignitaries, from Gandhi to Don Quixote. The newest sculptures were those of Adam and Eve, made of white Moscow stone. They lay on the ground, tormented by the forbidden fruit, but not yet expelled from the Garden of Eden. This was no Totalitarian Sculpture Garden, but something much more ordinary and pleasant.

This was a time when Russia had turned away from the project of examining its past. The new attitude toward Soviet history was one of nostalgia. The treatment of "monumental propaganda" was a preview of Russian propaganda to come: Its guiding principle is one of cacophony. Everything means nothing and something. Nothing is morally clear—not even Adam and Eve, who are neither here nor there but merely on the grass in front of a Moscow exhibit hall. Any story can be spun, but no one story—certainly not one as dramatic as the story of the word "Freedom!" painted on the monument to the founder of the Soviet secret police—can take hold.

I found the monument to Wallenberg in the courtyard of the Library of Foreign Literature. I knew this building well, though I had not been there in years. My mother had worked there in the 1970s, as an editor at a journal published by the library. Back then the library was run by Ludmila Kosygina, daughter of the Soviet prime minister. She largely left the intellectuals in her employ alone. One of those employees, a woman named Ekaterina Genieva, ran the library after the collapse of the Soviet Union, turning it into a cultural and intellectual hub. The library housed a British cultural center and an American one, and one of the first public internet centers funded by the American billionaire George Soros (who survived the Second World War in Budapest but was not one of the Jews helped by Wallenberg). Genieva died of cancer in June 2015, and the state immediately moved to shut down the free-wheeling, free-thinking programs at the library. Still, it made sense that a monument to Wallenberg would have found its home there.

Wedged on a triangular plot between a busy street and the Yauza River, the Library of Foreign Literature is an island. No one unintentionally stumbles into its courtyard, shielded by a tall iron gate. My first thought after I entered after a couple of decades' absence was, "I wish Svetlana Boym could see this." My friend had died several months earlier. She would have loved this sight. The courtyard was large—in my childhood it had been vast—and it was crowded with monuments. Thirty-one of them were there, sitting, striding, or standing. Most of them were life-size, and most were busts placed at eye level. This created the illusion of walking among people, as though at a cocktail party. Except the real party was a couple of miles from here, on the genteel lawn of the exhibit hall, while these were the outcasts, the ones who had no place alongside Dzerzhinsky or Adam and Eve. These were men who were too controversial to be placed out in the open in the city—like Yegor Gaidar, the first post-Communist prime minister and the engineer of Russian economic reforms, or Pope John Paul the Second. Some were irrelevant to the city, placed here simply because there was no street corner or patch of lawn for them to plant their podium. There was Heinrich Heine, Simón Bolívar, and Abraham Lincoln, gifted by the University of Illinois on the occasion of the library's seventy-fifth birthday. Charles Dickens was a gift from the BBC World Service. Niccolò Machiavelli was a gift from an Italian entrepreneur and signified the giver's "love for and respect of Russia," or so the plaque claimed. It was impossible to tell whether the entrepreneur had been trying to make a mockery of Russia, the library, or no one at all.

It seemed that the library courtyard had at some point become so much a repository of monuments that people communicated with the library by means of monuments, and the library responded in kind. There was a monument to Genieva, the library director who had died less than a year earlier. Her lifesize bronze likeness was descending the stairs of the main entrance. Staff and regular visitors entered by walking through the courtyard hardly noticing the monuments who crowded to either side of their passageway, and then encountered Genieva, who was now always there to greet them on the steps.

I walked among the men of stone and the woman of bronze and thought about death as a physical act. Death is located in space and time. Awareness of the circumstances of someone's death anchors the person's life in our memory. I knew where my mother had been when she died, and who had been with her. I knew where Svetlana had died, and who had held her hand. I even knew where Genieva had died, and who had sat by her bed. I knew which cancer had killed each of them.

Wallenberg's plaque said,

1912—?

He would have been a hundred and four now: His death was, finally, a fact. But it still had no known circumstance or specific cause.

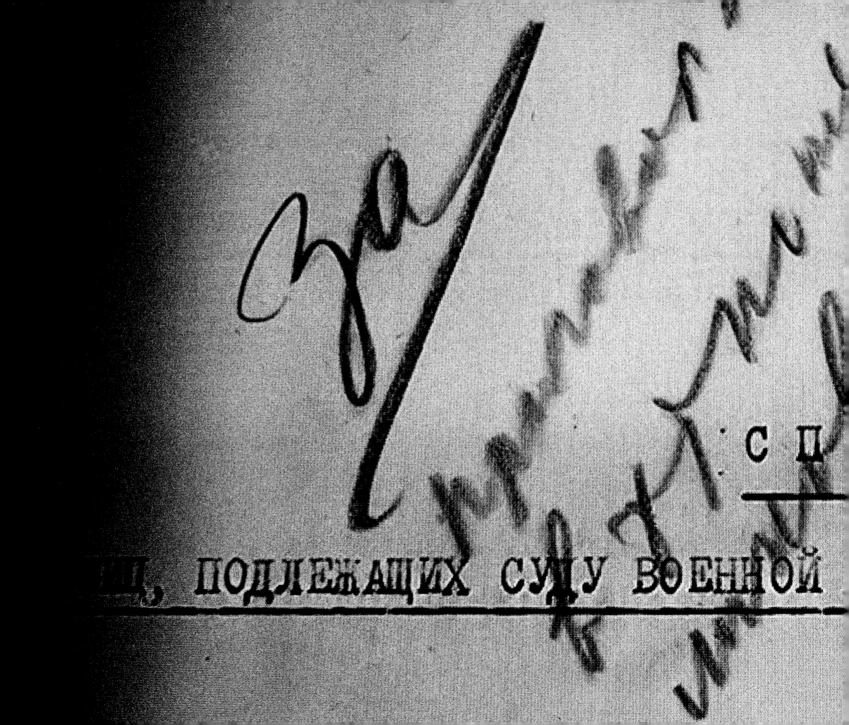

С П

Ц, ПОДЛЕЖАЩИХ СУДУ ВОЕННОЙ

СОК

ЛЛЕГИИ ВЕРХОВНОГО СУДА СОЮЗА ССР.

Евгения Яковлевна
Мустангова
1905—1937

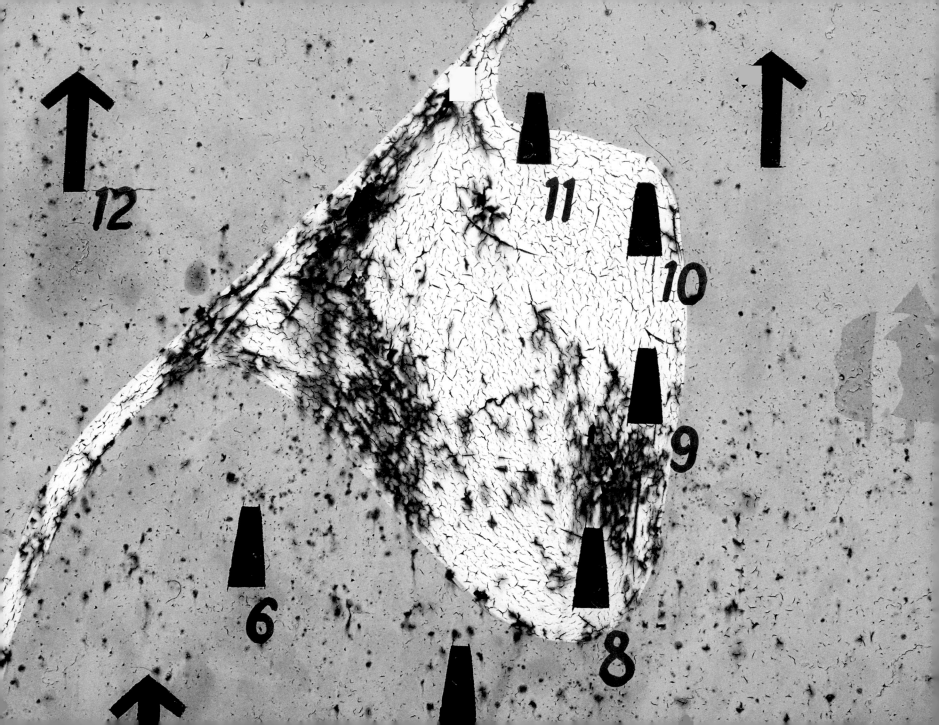

SANDARMOKH

PART ONE

The Bodies in the Forest

The death certificates could contain perhaps two truths and a lie, sometimes one truth and two lies. "Place of death" was always a lie. "Cause of death" was usually a lie—"heart failure," "pneumonia," nothing at all—but sometimes the truth: "Cause of death: execution." The one line that was most likely to be true was the one that indicated the date of death. There was no telling, though—often the paperwork claimed that a Gulag victim had lived long past the actual execution date. That was when there was any paperwork at all.

Writing about Soviet and Nazi camps in *The Origins of Totalitarianism,* Hannah Arendt described the unknown death as the ultimate assault on humanity.

The Western world has hitherto, even in its darkest periods, granted the slain enemy the right to be remembered as a self-evident acknowledgment of the fact that we are all men (and only men). It is only because even Achilles set out for Hector's funeral, only because the most despotic governments honored the slain enemy, only because the Romans allowed the Christians to write their martyrologies, only because the Church kept its heretics alive in the memory of men, that all was not lost and never could be lost. The concentration camps, by making death itself anonymous (making it impossible to find out whether a prisoner is dead or alive) robbed death of its meaning as the end of a fulfilled life. In a sense they took away the individual's own death, proving that henceforth nothing belonged to him and he belonged to no one. His death merely set a seal on the fact that he had never really existed.[i]

The early Memorial Societies looked for the bodies, the execution sites, the documents identifying the bodies—the truth. By restoring humanity posthumously, they hoped, perhaps, to restore humanity to the country itself. It seemed self-evident that once the facts were established, some sort of reckoning would have to follow. These memory activists knew even less about the world than they did about Russia's own history, but they had heard of de-Nazification, a policy and a campaign that seemed to have cleansed Germany of the legacy of totalitarianism. And perhaps because Germany had been both Russia's enemy and its counterpart, they did not give much thought to the circumstances of de-Nazification—not to the fact that the process had taken decades nor to the fact that the Germans had not chosen the policy for themselves but had had it forced upon them by the Allies. They just assumed that something like de-Communization would happen, and they assumed that accurate historical information—accurate factual memory—was a necessary condition; some even thought it would be a sufficient condition.

Thousands of people around the Soviet Union set off in search of facts, and bodies. Clues came from local lore—hushed tales of shots heard and cattle cars seen—and from the cryptic documents issued by Soviet authorities to the families of victims.

Nikolai Kovach started looking for his parents in 1953, the year Stalin died and Nikolai turned seventeen. He had grown up in an orphanage outside of Leningrad. When it was time for him to get his identity papers, the orphanage director instructed him to pick a patronymic—a derivative of the father's name that forms part of one's official identity. "You come from nowhere," the orphanage director said. "You have no parents." Kovach's objection was factual rather than existential: He could accept that there were people who "came from nowhere" but he knew that he was not one of those people. He had an unusual last name, and this meant that someone somewhere had to know something about him. He told the orphanage director

to put down "Ivanovich" for his patronymic—the Russian equivalent of "John Doe"—but once he became a trade-school student in Leningrad, he began filing information requests with the city office of internal affairs. "No information available" was the response he got. He continued filing his request every few years, for a total of five rejections.

In the novel *The Book of Laughter and Forgetting* Milan Kundera describes the bargain totalitarian regimes force on to their subjects:

They were ready to sell people a future in exchange for their past.... They wanted to compel him to cast his life away and become a shadow, a man without a past, an actor without a role, and to turn even his castaway life, even the role the actor had abandoned, into a shadow. Having turned him into a shadow, they would let him live.[ii]

Kovach, who was born in 1936, on the eve of the Great Terror, had spent his entire life as a shadow of a shadow. He had no way to imagine the bodies that had once cast those shadows. By the time I met him in 1997, he had come to believe that he had been subjected to a specific, circumscribed process.

"I was depersonalized," he told me.[iii]

It was not until 1956, three years after Stalin's death, that his successor Nikita Khrushchev denounced what he called the "cult of personality" and acknowledged that Stalin's thirty-year reign of political persecution had affected many "honest communists."[iv] He stopped far short of acknowledging that Stalin had unleashed state terror that had claimed millions of victims. Still, the speech signaled the release of most remaining political prisoners and the start

44 of a public conversation about the Gulag—albeit a brief and careful one. Uncounted Soviet citizens filed information requests with the authorities, inquiring after family members who had vanished five or ten or thirty years earlier. None of them learned the truth then, but some were handed small portions of fact, often in the form of a death certificate. The death certificates delivered shock, regret, and reassurance to different people in different measure.

After a few years, Khrushchev was deposed, the period known as the political "Thaw" ended, and talk of the Gulag was shut down. Alexander Solzhenitsyn, author of short stories about Gulag life that were published in Soviet magazines and a giant documentary novel about the Gulag that wasn't, was exiled from the country. Most people knew enough to stop looking for their vanished family members.

In the second half of the 1980s, *perestroika* and the accompanying policy of *glasnost*—openness—restarted a conversation about Stalinist terror. Victims' families—those of them who had survived and who had preserved an awareness of their loss for the second two decades of silence—began asking for information again. The new editions of Gulag death certificates tended to be more truthful than the previous issue, if truthfulness is a quality that can be measured in gradations. The new death certificates were less likely to disguise an execution as "heart failure" and more likely to contain a credible death date.

This was when Memorial Societies began their search. One of the logical places for them to start was Solovki, an archipelago in the White Sea where the first Soviet camp for political prisoners was located starting in 1923. It was the first, it was a literal archipelago, and several score of Russia's most prominent intellectuals had been interned there. It seemed right that the work of memory should begin at Solovki.

In 1989 Leningrad Memorial Society organized what they called Days of Memory at Solovki. Two of the leading organizers—fifty-one-year-old dissident and former political prisoner Veniamin Iofe and his twenty-nine-year-old assistant Irina Flige—boarded a traincar full of late-middle-age people (mostly women) whose parents (mostly fathers) had been inmates at Solovki. Between them, Iofe and Flige called their fellow travelers "the daughters." Most of the daughters were carrying their parents' freshly issued death certificates. Iofe asked to see them. He sat there, a stout, square-shouldered man with tightly curled gray hair and tiny spectacles, at a gray formica table in a train compartment, a glass of black tea in one hand and a stack of death certificates in the other.

"Look," he said. "This was a mass execution."

How did he know?

He showed her: Of the twenty death certificates in front of him, fifteen contained one of four dates of death, all within the same week in the fall of 1937. This was no coincidence, he said, and no statistical anomaly. It was a mass execution.

Strange, but this was the sort of thing that was making Flige fall in love with Iofe. She had known him since the late 1970s, first as an acquaintance of her father, then as an older comrade in the dissident movement. He had once taught her how to get accurate information about where the police were holding her friends. But now that they were working together, she was falling in love. It had to do with the way his mind brought the world into focus.

They knew that the camp at Solovki had been shut down in 1937, the year of the Great Terror. (The Bolsheviks had been ruling by terror since coming to power in 1917, and there had been show trials and executions before, but this was the year when thousands of people disappeared daily.) The inmates had been taken off the islands. Survivors' memoirs mentioned a mass execution, but Flige and Iofe were skeptical of such recollections: Memories carried in silence changed shape over decades. "Memoirs are not documents," was one of their rules. Now they were looking at documents that might be telling them that some or all of the inmates were executed soon after they left the islands—so soon, in fact, that they could hardly have been transported far from the archipelago. The executions were likely carried out on the mainland closest to Solovki. But where? There was still no way to know.

In 1991 Kovach, by then a retired military officer living in Leningrad, saw an ad in an all-classified local newspaper:

Looking for Nikolai Kovach, born 1936

He called. The number turned out to belong to a clerk at a local civil registry. She asked him to come to her office.

"I hope you don't faint," she said when he arrived. "Here is your sister's address. Go."

Kovach bought a bunch of flowers and went. The fifty-seven-year-old woman turned out to look a lot like him. His sister, Elena, was two years older than Kovach. She was three when they were separated, and she always remembered that she had a little brother.

Together over the next few years they managed to find out who their parents had been and what had happened to them. Their mother, Maria Astafyeva, was a Russian-born Chinese citizen—an exile—educated to be a lawyer. Their father, Karl Kovach, had been a high-level Bolshevik. They met when he was in China on official business. He asked the Soviet government for permission to marry Maria, but his request was denied, so Kovach disobeyed his orders. He was immediately called back to Moscow, and he returned with his new wife. They were arrested less than four months after arrival, in 1933. Both were convicted of espionage and sentenced to ten years of labor camps. At Solovki, they were allowed to live together. The children were born in the camp. In October 1937 the Kovachs were removed from the camp. Maria was executed immediately—date of death was November 1, 1937. Karl was sent to a camp in the Far East and executed there in 1938. The children were sent to different orphanages, stripped of their patronymics and dates of birth but allowed, for some reason or for no reason, to keep their last names, which enabled them to find each other fifty-four years later.

Maria's secret-police file contained a journal she kept for the first couple of months in the Soviet Union. She had been bitterly disappointed, it seemed, in her husband. She had fallen in love with another man. Two weeks after arriving in the country, she wrote, "Learn to suffer in silence. Learn to despise people who live by instinct alone."

Nikolai read the diary so many times that he memorized every line. He felt that he knew who he was now, because he knew who his parents were. Especially his mother, who was so much smarter than anyone he had ever met—there were references in her diary that he still didn't get—and still so much younger than he was. She was twenty-seven when she died. He wished he could visit her grave.

46   Unlike the Moscow Memorial members who were looking for Wallenberg, Flige and Iofe were never given unfettered access to any prison, camp, or court archives. They gained information through a series of accidents.

Their first break came in the early 1990s, when a local branch of the FSB—the successor agency to the KGB—started downsizing. A disgruntled former worker, an archivist, decamped with the protocols of the troikas—special three-person panels that passed speedy, extrajudicial verdicts. The protocols showed that troikas worked at Solovki in the summer of 1937, rubber-stamping death sentences. This confirmed the researchers' suspicion that there had been a mass execution of Solovki inmates in the fall of 1937.

The second break came in the mid 1990s. KGB archives in St. Petersburg (Leningrad had reverted to its old name after the collapse of the Soviet Union) remained largely inaccessible to researchers. But because Moscow Memorial Society had better luck, someone had the idea of filing an information request in the Russian capital. That yielded a document decreeing that several hundred inmates be removed from Solovki in the fall of 1937. The document contained a name: The man in charge of the operation was Captain Mikhail Matveev. The document also mentioned Medvezhya Gora—literally, Bear Mountain—the name of a town on the mainland. In the 1930s Medvezhya Gora was a Gulag capital, the headquarters for the construction of the White Sea Canal, a waterway dug by thousands of inmates.

In 1996 a retired secret-police officer published a memoir titled, unsubtly, *The Executioners Do Not Have Blood on Their Hands.* Iofe read it—he read everything. The book mentioned a Captain Matveev who seemed like he might be the person from the archival documents. It said that the captain had been awarded an engraved watch for his work but was later arrested.

This was a stroke of luck: Though the researchers did not have open access to the archives, as representatives of a nongovernmental organization they could request specific case files. Now that they knew that Matveev himself had been arrested, they could ask for his case.

Iofe and Flige went to the archives together—they had been married six years by now and had developed the habit of doing everything together. The case file showed that Matveev had been arrested for abuse of power. An archivist watched over Flige and Iofe as they read the file. They came back day after day, lugging a so-called portable copy machine with them. They had to make the case for copying each individual document, and the archivist ruled on their requests—many documents were not, for some reason or another, to be copied. It was a good thing there were two of them, though: They managed some sleight of hand.

They pieced together the story. Matveev had been instructed to remove 1,116 inmates from Solovki and carry out their death sentences "in the usual location." He encountered logistical difficulties. He needed transport, but there was none. The Gulag authorities in Medvezhya Gora gave him tires—the best, they claimed, that they could do—so he would be able to exchange the tires for the use of a truck. When they got to this part, Iofe and Flige concluded that they were dealing with authentic case documents: No one would have made this stuff up.

In the end, Matveev had use of one truck and one car. He also had ten assistants, two of whom drove the vehicles, and the use of a wooden barracks too small to house all the inmates. They never figured out exactly where he put the inmates while they were still alive, but the rest of the story was fairly clear.

He began on October 27, by taking about twenty people to the execution site; he used the truck, which could fit sixteen, to transport men, while the women were driven in the passenger car. On that first day, one of the inmates succeeded in untying or perhaps even cutting (had he secreted a knife?) the rope binding his hands, and attempted to escape. Matveev and his helpers stopped him and proceeded to execute the inmates as planned, but the near-break gave them a scare. Matveev halted the executions. For the next few days, he drank and thought about ways to carry out the operation. The work resumed on November 1.

Matveev had devised a new procedure and designed a new implement: a wooden bat for hitting inmates. The process now involved a sequence of three interconnected rooms in the barracks. In Room 1, an inmate's identity was checked against a list, then the inmate was stripped to his or her underwear and searched. In Room 2, the inmate's hands and feet were bound with rope. In Room 3, the inmate was rendered unconscious with a blow of Matveev's special bat to the back of the head.

Unconscious inmates could be stacked, which raised the truck's capacity to forty people. The stack was draped with a tarpaulin, and Matveev's assistants sat on top, special bat at the ready in case anyone regained consciousness. The new system was efficient: Matveev's work was done on November 4. On November 10, he submitted his final report. He had carried out 1,111 death sentences; one inmate had died before he could be executed and four had been transported to other prisons, presumably because their sentences had been changed.[vi]

The precision of Matveev's reporting made his central omission that much more obvious. The executioners documented everything, it seemed, except for the locations of the executions. Of that, Matveev said only that the location chosen by his superiors—whatever the initial orders referred to as "the usual"—was objectionable because of its proximity to a village, which made it difficult to keep the executions secret.

But why did the executions need to be secret? If state terror was the Bolsheviks' chosen tool of governing, if frightening the population into paralysis was Stalin's way of securing power in perpetuity, then shouldn't they want to carry out the executions in the public square? Instead, they fired their shots under cover of night. Matveev and other Soviet executioners always indicated the precise time of their actions in their reports: two, three, four in the morning. Iofe and Flige grew convinced that the time was supplied as additional proof of secrecy: It had been dark, and no one saw it happen.

After reading hundreds of Great Terror cases, Flige formed a theory about the need for secrecy. These cases—skinny file folders—could easily run together in one's mind, because of how little identifying information they contained. It was like reading the same sad, formulaic book over and over again. But then Flige stopped to consider the plot of this book. It contained two people. One, the victim, was invariably convinced that he had been arrested by mistake. Whatever the charges—espionage, treason, terrorism—he found them unthinkable, as far outside the realm of normality as anything could be. But his interrogator's job was to force the victim to confess, whether it was to spying for a foreign power, plotting to overthrow the government, or planning to assassinate Stalin. The interrogator almost never failed to force a

48 confession. The interrogator spent his days and nights—for the terror machine churned around the clock—facing people who, he was convinced, wanted an end to the Bolshevik state. At some point he would have had to start feeling that wanting to kill Stalin or to blow up the secret police was normal. On some level, then, he had to feel that the state he served and the way he served it were illegitimate. No wonder the killing of enemies of the state had to be kept secret then.

Matveev's copious reports indicated that the execution site was nineteen kilometers from the barracks. Flige and Iofe used a compass to draw a circle on a map. There were a lot of roads heading out of town: the execution site could be anywhere. Then they came across a report in which Matveev described the mechanical failure of one of his vehicles. He had been in a panic: the truck full of condemned people, still alive, had been forced to stop just outside a village called Pindushi. That narrowed the search down to a single road out of Medvezhya Gora.

In July 1997 Iofe and Flige took an overnight train from St. Petersburg to Medvezhya Gora. A local official arranged for a military unit stationed nearby to send conscripts to help with a dig. Flige and Iofe were joined by Yuri Dmitriev, the head of Memorial Society in the nearest large city, Petrozavodsk.

The soldiers were digging trenches and getting bored. Dmitriev wandered off into the forest. Then he reappeared.

"I think I found it," he said.

A short distance from where they had been digging, the ground—if one looked carefully—did not look normal. It dipped and rose, like the bottom of the sea. But it was the shape of the depressions that was particularly striking: they were large rectangles.

The soldiers had dug down about six feet—their heads were just below ground level—when they jumped out as though they had been bitten. They had hit bone.

The soldiers said that they would not go back down. They were kids—eighteen or nineteen years old—and they were terrified. Flige hopped into the pit. She was trained in archaeological digging: She had the brushes and the skills to clean away the soil and get a clear view of the stacks of bodies. Except that this was no archaeological dig. For the forty minutes that she was in the pit, she thought about the people whose remains she might now be touching. They had names. She had met their children and grandchildren.

The bodies lay on top of one another, their heads facing in the same direction. The skulls had bullet holes in them. The way Matveev did it was this: The inmates were tossed into the deep rectangular pits; Matveev stood in the pit and shot each person in the head with a handgun. When he was done, he climbed out, using the bodies like a set of stairs.

Now what? They had been in the memory business for years, but they had never actually found an execution site before. Dmitriev wanted to open up every one of the pits, exhume the remains, document the means of execution, catalog every body. Flige was opposed. For better or for worse, these people were buried here now. Taking them out would, among other things, inevitably mean mixing up the bones. That seemed cruel. They should be allowed their resting place, such as it was. It also seemed unnecessary: What was the point of cataloging every hipbone or even every skull? When Dmitriev was out of earshot, she called his preoccupation "necrophilia." Though she had to acknowledge that many of those who were looking for execution sites all over the former Soviet Union shared his passion for counting.

They settled on not disturbing the bodies. Still, they had to find all the pits and mark them. There were depressions in the ground as far as they could see. Flige and Iofe went into town and bought wooden fencing planks and red nail polish—the closest thing to a permanent marker that they could find. Flige painted numbers on the planks, and the three of them wandered, sticking planks into the ground where they found a rectangular depression. Whenever they ran out of depressions, their count would be complete. They stopped at two hundred and thirty-six.

They called in the authorities: the prosecutor's office, because this was the site of a mass murder; the forestry service, because this was in the woods; the local administration, because the remains of hundreds of people were found on its territory. The prosecutors debated the terms with Flige. Were there *mass* casualties, as she was insisting, or merely *multiple* ones? They opened up a couple more pits to make sure that they too were filled with bodies. They took two skulls for inspection, and it was then that Flige found herself losing it: she screamed at them that they needed to mark the skulls to know which pit they came from, and they stared at her like the words she said held no meaning, like which skull was attached to which pit held no meaning. The forestry workers were the opposite: they seemed shell-shocked. One of them kept saying that he had always gone mushroom-picking here. It was like 1,111 bodies had been found in his backyard. The locals had always said that the depressions were caused by bombs dropped during the Second World War—as though bombs could cause rectangular pits.

The regional government scheduled a memorial ceremony for October 27, 1997—the sixtieth anniversary of the first of Matveev's days of execution. They began building a road. This was going to be a big event.

In addition to a road, a memorial needed to be constructed. What should it be like? This was Year Eighty since the Bolshevik revolution, Year Sixty since the Great Terror, Year Forty-One since Khrushchev's takedown of the cult of personality, Year Seven since the collapse of the Soviet Union—and this was to be the first memorial erected with government sanction at a known execution site. The original assumptions on which Memorial Societies had been founded—that facts would bring a reckoning—had long since been debunked. Glasnost in the 1980s had allowed the publication of a wealth of archival information, a number of former inmates' memoirs, and *The Gulag Archipelago* itself. But after the USSR dissolved in 1991, the Russian public's focus shifted to its dramatic and traumatic present. Nor was Boris Yeltsin's government invested in examining the country's past: Consensus among the Russian powerful was that history was not particularly interesting but was potentially explosive. What if people found out, as they almost certainly would have, that their neighbors, or their neighbors' parents, had denounced, imprisoned, tortured, or executed their parents? The Russian government believed it was better to move forward without excavating the past literally or figuratively. So the secret police remained the gatekeeper of the archives—which was why it was only a series of coincidences that allowed Flige and Iofe to find this site.

That the regional government was now eager to build a memorial was something of an accident. Iofe thought that this might be because this region had an unusually high ratio of victims to perpetrators—to the extent that one could be separated from the other—because of the White Sea Canal and because the region had been a site of internal exile.[vii] Dmitriev, the local Memorial leader, confirmed Iofe's theory: There were villages in these parts, he said, where fewer people had died in the course of the Second World War than had been killed during the Great Terror.[viii]

Flige and Iofe brought in an artist to design a memorial. He was taken with the fencing planks that Flige and Iofe had used to mark the pits, so he decided to make them permanent. He designed plain wooden markers with something like a tiny gable roof on each. They looked a bit like miniature bell towers. From a distance, they looked like they might be wooden graveyard crosses. Cultural historian Alexander Etkind later observed that they looked like "a human figure with hands raised in prayer."[ix] The St. Petersburg team envisioned the markers as a way to enable the victims' descendants to create their own memorials, too: On opening day they would hand out pencils to allow people to write names on the markers. It was important that the markers were not crosses. The 1,111 victims included a large number of of people of Jewish and Muslim origin—though most of them, being Bolsheviks, would have been atheists—as well as groups of both Orthodox and Catholic clergy.

The local Orthodox church wanted to build a chapel at the site. The administration agreed, but by now it was autumn—how could one be constructed so fast? They found a carpenter who specialized in saunas. He built a wooden chapel in three weeks. The head of the Catholic church in St. Petersburg wanted a Catholic cross on the site. The administration agreed. But then the Orthodox church wanted a cross too, in addition to the chapel. A battle of the crosses ensued. In the end, both the Orthodox and Catholic crosses were placed in the same clearing. The Orthodox cross was a few inches taller—this had been a matter of principle—but the Catholic cross happened to be placed on a tiny hillock, which made it look taller.

All of this seemed too understated to Dmitriev, too silent. He commissioned a stone monument with an inscription. Here he and the St. Petersburg researchers ran into the perennial problem of counting. There was no way to tell how many people had been killed here. Flige and Iofe had 1,111 names tied to specific execution dates. But there were clearly more bodies here. With two hundred and thirty-six pits, there had to be more than two thousand, probably a lot more, perhaps more than five thousand. The fact that Matveev had been instructed to carry out the executions "in the usual location" indicated that people had been killed here before the 1,111 Solovki inmates and, possibly, after. Flige and Iofe remained opposed to exhuming and counting the bones, especially because this would yield nothing but a body count: there was no way to tell who these people had been and when they were killed. Flige and Iofe insisted on sticking with the known facts. A simple stone monument that they commissioned says, "Between 27 October and 4 November 1937, 1,111 inmates of the Solovki Prison were executed here." This stone sits to the right of the road leading to the site.

But to Dmitriev, sticking to the known facts amounted to underreporting. Directly opposite the stone commissioned by Flige and Iofe sits a larger stone that he commissioned:

Here in the Sandarmokh canyon, the site of mass executions between the years 1934 and 1941, more than 7,000 entirely innocent people were killed. They were residents of Karelia, inmates of the White Sea Canal Camp, inmates of the Solovki Prison. Remember us, people! Do not kill one another!

Flige disliked everything about this message. Why say "entirely innocent"? How was one to know if the people who had been stripped, knocked unconscious, stacked, and shot here were innocent? Why did it matter? And what were they supposed to be innocent of? They were accused of crimes against the Soviet state. Some of them had indeed opposed the state. Would that have made them less than entirely innocent, or more deserving of the fate that they suffered here? Why would one even want to assert innocence in the face of such an accusation now, sixty years later? Iofe, for one, wore his 1965 conviction for "anti-Soviet propaganda" with pride.

The St. Petersburg and local activists' approaches clashed, perhaps, because their roles did. Flige and Iofe, though neither was trained as an academic, saw their mission as one of documenting only that which could be known. Dmitriev was an activist whose commitment was to people rather than facts. He did not disrespect facts, but on the rare occasions when he had to choose, his allegiance was to people. These people came to him in search of memory, specifically in search of the place where their family members had been buried. Sometimes, perhaps often, Dmitriev told them that their loved ones may have been killed at Sandarmokh. When I interviewed Dmitriev in 1997, he believed that the site contained the remains of 2,341 local residents and 2,400 White Sea Canal inmates, in addition to the 1,111 Solovki inmates. That would have been 5,852 people. Within a few months, he had raised his estimate to more than 7,000. By the time Etkind was writing in the early 2000s, the figure given to him by Dmitriev was 9,000.[x]

Etkind observed that Dmitriev was unusual not merely among memory activists but among Russian citizens generally in that he had no discernible family connection to the history of terror. He was the child of neither victims nor perpetrators nor, like many people, both. But his partners in the local Memorial were different.

Dmitriev was supported by Ivan Chukhin, whose father was an NKVD officer who was implicated in the terror, and Pertti Vuori, whose father was murdered in 1936 by the same NKVD in Karelia. It was a remarkable team: a descendant of a victim, a descendant of a perpetrator, and a third party, as neutral to the subject as it is possible to be.[xi]

I would add that Chukhin was a former police officer himself; his was a Soviet law-enforcement family. Chukhin died in a car accident shortly before the execution site at Sandarmokh was found. Vuori died soon after, also as a young man. That left Dmitriev, who perhaps saw his legacy as one of mediation, of giving voice to the dead who had been silenced while still alive. At least that's how he made sense of the deaths at Sandarmokh, as though the bones themselves screamed out: "People, don't kill one another."

Of course, the executioners at Sandarmokh—Matveev and his assistants—though they were known by name, were not "people": They were the Soviet state. To underscore this, Memorial activists have insisted on using the word "terror"—state terror. The Russian state has preferred the term "repressions," or "mass repressions," which dates back to Khrushchev's 1956 speech. The word "terror" emerged in the public sphere during glasnost, but ultimately lost the

52 battle to "repressions." *Terror* connotes an active perpetrator: the criminal state itself. *Repressions* seem to have happened of their own accord, like a force of nature that swept through, leaving a ravaged country in its wake. On the subject of terror—the word—Dmitriev, Flige, and Iofe saw eye to eye. Dmitriev included the word in his text for the monument, but it was apparently excised by the engravers.

The commemorative ceremony was held on October 27, 1997, as planned—or almost as planned. The British historian Catherine Merridale described what she saw:

If you are accustomed to Soviet-style, open-air meetings, you will be used to standing around and watching people whose hearts and minds are entirely disengaged from the performance they are about to give. It was common knowledge, in the Soviet era, that the measure of a good public gathering was the quality of the sandwiches and vodka that followed it. There was something of this in the air that morning, something dishonest, or impatient, at least, about the large men in suits and furs as they prepared to give their megaphone public speeches. The church authorities were there, and the town council, provincial politicians, and even representatives of the Duma in Moscow. There were human-rights activists, media intellectuals, and representatives from the national government of newly independent Ukraine and Belarus. Whatever they had expected, they were about to be surprised.

Just as the first speaker was preparing his text, a woman in a black woolen shawl began to wail and wring her hands in the snow a few yards from the tribune. As she threw herself onto the frozen ground, another joined her, and then more. The sound they were making was the unearthly poetry of lament. A hundred years ago, this wailing would

have accompanied every death and continued for days. Funerals were neither solemn nor silent. What we were hearing was not a revived tradition. Karelia is remote, and there are women there who had never learned to behave like discreet Soviet mourners beside a family grave. They wept for their lost husbands; they described the lifelong search that was about to end, the bitter years through which they longed to find the grave that they soon hoped to share. The city men coughed uneasily and looked around for security. Eventually, someone began to move the women away, and the crowd closed over the places they had claimed.[xii]

I was there too that day. My notes add some detail:

Before the official ceremony can begin, an old woman falls to her knees by the stone that marks entry to the burial ground and begins wailing: "I was searching for you for so long, my dear papa! My dear mama didn't live long enough to see you!" Several other old women join in the wailing. One of the organizers tries to calm them: "Granny, you'll be walking around and you'll find his grave and you'll feel better. Your heart will tell you where he lies." Eventually, the ceremony gets started, but then the wailing resumes: "My dear papa, my only one, you left us six children. My dear papa, you came to me in my dream and you said, 'I'm naked.'"

There was snow on the ground, as there would have been on this day sixty years ago. These old people imagined their young parents in the snow in their underwear. Merridale was mistaken: these were not wives but daughters and sons. Most of them were in their sixties, but they had lived lives of grief, fear, and hunger, and they were old. Nikolai Kovach was there alone. His older sister Elena was no longer well enough to make the trip. He had brought his mother's journal with him and later read to me from it in his hotel room but wouldn't let me look for myself—he said that it was too personal.

At the ceremony, local officials spoke and so did Dmitriev, and so did an Orthodox and then a Catholic priest. The families used pencils and ballpoint pens to write names on the wooden markers. Most of them had brought plastic flowers or funeral wreaths, which they now placed next to the markers they had claimed. I found a small stone in the snow and placed it on the large stone at the entrance. A couple of people gave me puzzled looks. I was probably the only person here who knew that Jews place stones, not flowers, in memory of their dead.

Though this was the first time an actual execution site was recognized with an officially sanctioned monument, the markers, crosses, and stones of Sandarmokh were not the first attempt at memorializing Soviet terror. Other attempts at memorialization had been either abstracted—placed in symbolic locations rather than at execution sites—or installed without official sanction. One could imagine that Sandormokh was a breakthrough and a slightly belated beginning of a new era of remembrance. The remains of millions of people hidden in plain sight all over the former empire had to be given their markers, monuments, museums.

This did not happen. Twenty years later, the memorial at Sandarmokh is unique. The work of remembering the Soviet dead ended almost as soon as it had begun. Less than two years after the Sandarmokh memorial opening, Vladimir Putin, a former lieutenant colonel in the KGB, came to power in Russia, his popularity driven in large part by a campaign of nostalgia for an imaginary heroic, happy, and orderly Soviet past. Talk of Stalinist terror became increasingly unfashionable and even unpatriotic. Books extolling Stalin and Stalinism became, first, possible and then popular. Memorial Society branches all over the country came under pressure. When Putin began a political crackdown following popular protests in 2012, Memorial was singled out for attack and eventually declared a "foreign agent."

In St. Petersburg, Flige managed in part by moving some Memorial activities into a new organization, the Veniamin Iofe Memorial Foundation. Her husband had died of a heart attack on the afternoon of April 20, 2002, while riding the escalator at the Bolshevik Prospect metro station in St. Petersburg. When Flige wrote the introduction to a posthumous collection of his essays, she noted the fact that he had died on an escalator—it was her habit to note the exact location of a death—but omitted the name of the station, perhaps because the absurdity of linking the word *Bolshevik* to Iofe's memory would have been too painful.[xiii] It had been more than a decade since Russia stopped removing Communist-era monuments and changing Communist-era location names: They had long since faded into the background, once again becoming an unremarkable part of the landscape.

When I visited Flige at the office of the Veniamin Iofe Memorial Foundation in 2016, I told her I was writing a book about forgetting, to which remembering had ceded so easily. She told me I was wrong.

"It's not that we are witnessing the process of forgetting—it's that we had our bearings wrong in the first place. We thought we were constructing historical memory. But historical memory can exist only when there is a clear line separating the present from the past. That's when you can say, 'After the Holocaust,' for example.

54   But we don't have that break—there is no past, only a continuous present. As long as that's the case, we are talking about legacy rather than memory: the continuing legacy of an experience we so cavalierly relegated to the past. That was a mistake. We really wanted it to be true, we really wanted to be like Germany, so we just decided that it was true."

       Back then, in the 1990s, people like Flige were talking about "de-Communization," which they imagined would be like de-Nazification. But twenty years later, she was telling me that I was wrong to talk about forgetting because forgetting presupposes remembering—and remembering had not happened, or had not happened yet. It was an extraordinary statement coming from a woman who had spent most of her adult life running an organization called the Memorial Society. After nearly three decades, she had come to the conclusion that the time for memory had not yet come. If anything, that made her work all that much more urgent: She was preserving facts, images, and objects for a future in which the work of memory may finally begin.

The Last Daughter

Of all the children of Sandarmokh victims who attended the 1997 memorial opening, only one was still living and in Russia twenty years later. Elizaveta Delibash had spent her life trying to piece together the story of her parents. To begin with, she remembered little.

She is eight years old. She and her mother live in a small room where the walls are made of rough-hewn boards. They sleep on a wooden platform that's bolted to the wall. There is a bookshelf in the room, two or three stools, and a rickety table. Elizaveta's father visits them in this room, but he doesn't live here. One day, three men enter. They are dressed unlike any of the people Elizaveta is used to seeing. Their uniforms look new, their boots are shined, and they are wearing holsters with criss-crossed leather shoulder belts. They start grabbing books off the shelf and throwing them to the floor. Elizaveta's mother leans over her.

"Quiet, quiet."

"But they shouldn't be doing this! They are throwing books on the floor!"

"Quiet, quiet."

Then Elizaveta's father is there, then the other men lead him out of the room. When he returns, there is blood coming out of the corner of his mouth.

"Mama, papa is bleeding."

"Quiet, quiet, it's just his TB."

Then the men lead both of her parents out. And then Elizaveta is on a train. She has her own suitcase with her as well as her mother's, but her mother is not there. There is a woman Elizaveta doesn't know. She has told her, "I'm taking you to your family in Leningrad." There are bars on the windows in this train, and a soldier with a rifle guarding them. When they arrive, he helps carry the two suitcases.

56 *The woman takes her to a large building, up the stairs. There is a man who looks familiar. "Her grandmother is dead," he tells the woman, but he takes the suitcases and brings Elizaveta into the apartment.*

The man was Elizaveta's father's stepfather. He later told her that the woman who brought her had said, "I'm not going to tell you my name, but we have decided that this girl, the daughter of a good man, should survive."

Elizaveta's father, Alexander Iosilevich, had been a Bolshevik. He had joined the underground revolutionary movement as a fifteen-year-old. After the revolution, he became an officer of the Soviet secret police; he was nineteen. He quit eight years later, in 1926, and was arrested in 1927. He was expelled from the Party and sentenced to three years' exile in Siberia for libeling the secret police. He was released early but then rearrested in 1930 and sentenced to ten years of prison camps for anti-Soviet activities.[xiv]

Elizaveta was born during her father's Siberian exile. Her mother's name was Nina Delibash. She was an actress and, as Elizaveta was able to confirm decades later when she saw a photograph of her, a stunningly beautiful woman. Nina was arrested in 1930, in connection with her husband's arrest, and sentenced to three years of Siberian exile. Relatives took care of her daughter but were scared to give Nina herself shelter after she was released. She found a job at the camp where her husband was interned. That room that Elizaveta remembered was at Solovki, where Nina worked—perhaps as a teacher, or as an entertainer. She was re-arrested that day in April 1936. Elizaveta was never able to learn who took care of her at the camp after that and who figured out a way to smuggle her out.

Eight-year-old Elizaveta needed to be hidden in Leningrad. Otherwise she might be taken away to an orphanage for "children of enemies of the people." Or she could draw attention to her relatives, who would then risk arrest. She spent two weeks on a tiny cot behind a curtain in her father's brother's room in a communal apartment, then another couple of weeks behind another curtain, in her mother's sister's room. Then two other maternal aunts boarded a train to Georgia with her. They went all the way to the border with Turkey. Her maternal grandparents lived in a village there. That is, they lived on what used to be their farm—now it was part of a collective farm. It was far from the nearest town. At first Elizaveta's grandparents' friends agreed to have the girl stay with them in town so she could attend school, but her nightmares kept them up every night and they canceled the arrangement. Back in Leningrad, two of Elizaveta's maternal aunts were arrested, as was one of her paternal uncles. Elizaveta herself disappeared into her grandparents' house. For the next four years they taught her at home. After that, her grandmother, a former schoolteacher, said that she needed to attend a proper middle school.

One of Elizaveta's maternal aunts—the only one of her mother's sisters who remained free—said that the girl could come and live in Leningrad with her and her two daughters. The girls' father had been executed; their mother had remarried, but her new husband was currently under arrest. The aunt always had a bag packed in case they came for her. They didn't. In fact, one after another, their relatives returned: the two aunts, one surviving uncle, and her aunt's husband. The husband said that he had spent the year in a cell so crowded that only some of the inmates could lie down at a time and then they were packed so tightly on the floor that they could turn only if they all did it at once.

Things felt better—more settled—when the aunts and uncles came home. Only one uncle and Elizaveta's parents were missing. Then the war began. They were lucky enough to be evacuated from Leningrad, which would soon be under siege. They were taken east and placed in a village with no people, only empty houses. Later Elizaveta realized that all the residents had been deported. After a year, they were starving. Elizaveta's aunt sold everything, even things from Elizaveta's mother's suitcase, which no one had disturbed in six years, and then she was desperate. She managed to get permission to put the three girls on a Georgia-bound military train. They traveled for a month, three girls aged sixteen, fourteen, and twelve. They lived with their grandfather until the end of the war and then returned to Leningrad.

Elizaveta graduated from university in 1952 with a degree in philology. She was invited to stay on for graduate study, but an acquaintance advised her to leave town: A new wave of arrests was underway. She got a job in the city of Krasnodar in southern Russia.

Stalin died in 1953, and Elizaveta returned to Leningrad. She was married now, to her paternal grandmother's stepson, who was barely out of his teens. It seemed almost inevitable that she would have married within her extended family: Staying inside was safer for her and for others. Her husband was Jewish. Stalin's last round of purges had been aimed against the Jews. Stalin was dead and the mass arrests had stopped, but the anti-Semitic policies remained. Between that and being the daughter of "enemies of the people," Elizaveta could not find a job teaching school in Leningrad—despite a shortage of teachers with college degrees. She eventually found work at a library and, later, as an editor at a publishing house that specialized in books about the cinema.

In 1956, after Khrushchev's big speech, she went to the secret police to ask for information on her parents. She knew—or at least she assumed—that her father had been executed. But what had happened to her mother? Elizaveta had two letters from her mother that she had carried everywhere with her. One said, "At night, look at the sky and find the North Star. Know that I am looking at it too, and thinking about you." This letter was in an envelope that had Solovki as the return address. The second was a note that had apparently been thrown out a train window—people did that, and others picked up the scraps of paper and mailed them. This one said, "I'm dying. Please save my daughter."

The officer at the secret police headquarters in Leningrad told Elizaveta that her parents' convictions would not be overturned but that she could go to the registry office and request her parents' death certificates. Death certificates? Somehow, Elizaveta had thought that her mother was still alive. She had been guilty of nothing! True, her father was guilty of nothing as well, but still, these were the words she used speaking to me sixty years later: "We thought that, being just a wife, my mother was guilty of nothing and might be alive."

The death certificate gave June 1941 as her mother's date of death and had a large Z through the lines where location of death and cause of death would have been indicated.

In addition to the death certificate, Elizaveta had the two letters from her mother. She had no pictures of her mother but two of her father. In one, he was baby-faced, with a round head of curls, a boy wearing a pince-nez and a tie. In another he was barely older, pictured with two comrades. They are wearing revolutionary garb—a belted peasant shirt on one, a leather trench coat on the other—but

58 Elizaveta's father is dressed like a dandy, in a three-piece suit, tie, collar pin, and holding a lit cigarette with a long line of ash—he has been waiting still for the photographer.

There had been more pictures, but Elizaveta's grandparents had burned them. Elizaveta kept the album with the gray felt cover and carried it with her every time she moved, but it had no photographs inside. Pictures could be dangerous, as could reminiscences. The grandparents refused to answer questions about Elizaveta's parents, and she knew why: They feared that if she knew something, she would say something. By the time it was safe to talk, Elizaveta's grandparents were gone. She went to see her mother's younger sister in the town where she lived.

"I remember nothing," the woman said.

"But it's safe now," Elizaveta told her. "You can tell me."

"I remember nothing."

Elizaveta resumed her search in 1988, during glasnost. It took years of filing requests and going into archives, where she was allowed to copy information by hand but not to make photocopies, to assemble a picture of what had happened to her parents. Alexander Iosilevich was executed in a jail in the city of Gorky on May 19, 1937. He had been thirty-eight. There was no information about the location of his remains. Nina Delibash was executed on November 2, 1937. She had been thirty-four. She was shot at Sandarmokh. It had been the third day of Captain Matveev's executions—Nina was among those who were first stripped to their underwear and bound, then rendered unconscious with a blow of the bat to the back of the head.

Elizaveta completed her search in 2011. She went to the opening of the Sandarmokh memorial in 1997 and went to the annual memorial ceremony there every year after, until 2014. After that, the trip became too taxing. She was in her eighties now.

Elizaveta Delibash's search for information about her parents led her to Memorial Society, where she started working full-time once she retired in 1992. She helped in Flige and Iofe's search that ultimately led to the site of her own mother's execution. Her personal project became a project of preservation, meticulous and factual. It is the most difficult way of remembering, because it offers no solace, no sense-making that would dangle the possibility of finding peace with the past, and of seeing it as the past. "Terror has no positive meaning or function," writes Etkind. "The assertion of any such function borders on justifying the enormous suffering of its victims."[xv] But that means that the victims died for nothing in every sense: for no reason—they were "guilty of nothing"—and for no purpose. This is a very difficult position to assert and maintain.

Indeed, much as Elizaveta tries to stick to the facts when she tells me about her findings, narratives keep emerging—stories she has composed with the information she found. Like when she got the case files that showed that at a certain point her mother stopped writing to Stalin to ask for mercy for her husband, who, she had been writing, was innocent. She started writing, instead, that Alexander was guilty but she herself was not and should be spared. "She must have known that he had been executed," Elizaveta says. Or if she didn't, she suggests, then perhaps her mother was tortured.

Her only photograph of her mother comes from a case file: it is tiny and closely cropped. She remembers other photographs from before they were burned, and she even has a picture of the man who took them all: her paternal uncle Victor, a cameraman.

He is handsome, with a flashy mustache. He was the only one of four brothers to avoid arrest in the 1930s, but he was arrested briefly after the war, for a crime of moral turpitude. Legend has it, Stalin ordered her uncle released because he admired the man's camerawork.

A crime of moral turpitude?

"It was ridiculous," says Elizaveta. "He was married. Though they had no children."

Before I fully realize that her uncle was arrested for homosexual contact, Elizaveta moves on. My efforts to return her to the topic of her uncle Victor's arrest are futile. Of all the arrests and executions she has described, this is the one that she finds impossible to assimilate. It is too shameful to fit in a story.

The stubborn lack of interpretation that Etkind suggests as the only appropriate way of remembering the terror is difficult to fix in stone, wood, or bronze. A monument is always the expression of an understanding of an event or a person, the story we tell about a person's life or death, or about a battle or a tragedy. But what if the event defies understanding? What if no sense can be made of it, or worse, what if making sense of it would serve to deny its most important feature, which is that it cannot be understood? Flige and Iofe and the artist they originally engaged for Sandarmokh tried to show the inexpressible nature of the terror in the wooden markers: neither crosses nor monuments, they were not symbols of either heroism or peace. But resistance to such a stark approach began before the memorial even opened, with the chapel and the two crosses and the stone with its call for "people" to stop "killing one another." It continued when relatives, in the days after the opening, began affixing photographs of victims to trees. They were trying to personalize the memorial, to assert the humanity of their loved ones—but also, in effect, to deny the impersonal nature of state terror.

The tension between acknowledging the humanity of the victims and the dehumanizing nature of the killing machines lies at the heart of every Holocaust memorial in the world. A small army of curators, artists, and architects have for decades been designing spaces that show both faces and facelessness. But Sandarmokh has no curator. It has no architect, and it has no guards. Since the opening in 1997, it has slowly turned into a spontaneous memorial continuously created and recreated by dozens of different people and groups.

I went to Sandarmokh for the second time in the spring of 2016. A sign on the highway pointed to the "Sandarmokh burial grounds." There was scarcely more explanation at the site itself: It was hard to imagine what an accidental visitor would make of it—but then, it was hard to imagine an accidental visitor here, nineteen kilometers from the very small town of Medvezhya Gora.

There are now hundreds of memorials at Sandarmokh: crosses, stones, plaques. Many of them contain photographs and names. Most contain the word "memory." Only one contains the word "terror." The monuments stretch nearly as far as the eye can see from most spots at the site. The ground there looks like waves in the snow—snow is on the ground most of the year. Each depression is a pit in which an unknown number of people were shot. These depressions are the literal opposite of graves—they dip below ground rather than rise above it—but some of the monument makers have constructed pseudograves by creating mounds, placing crosses on them, and in some cases even putting a small fence around the hillocks. This is done with graves at Russian graveyards, where survivors stake out private spaces for grieving.

60   Indeed, with the crosses, the stones, the fences, and a variety
of wreaths and scores of red plastic carnations as though sprout-
ing from the snow, this place, with every passing year, looks more
and more like a graveyard. This is almost exactly what Flige and Iofe
were trying to avoid, but the urge to mourn, to "find the grave and
feel better," as the wailing old woman was encouraged to do back in
1997, has overwhelmed their best efforts.

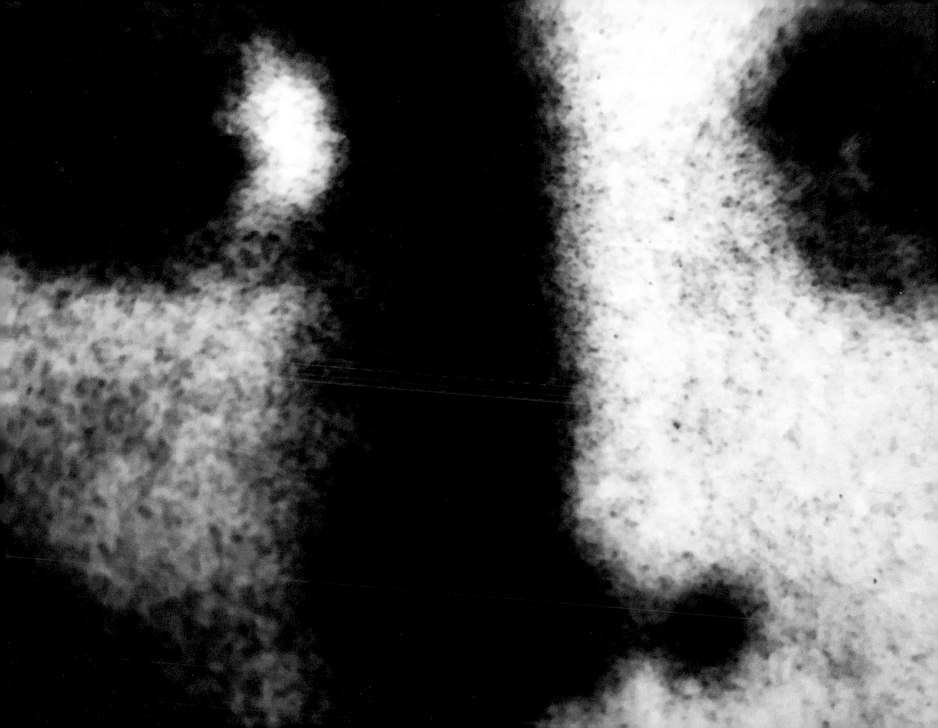

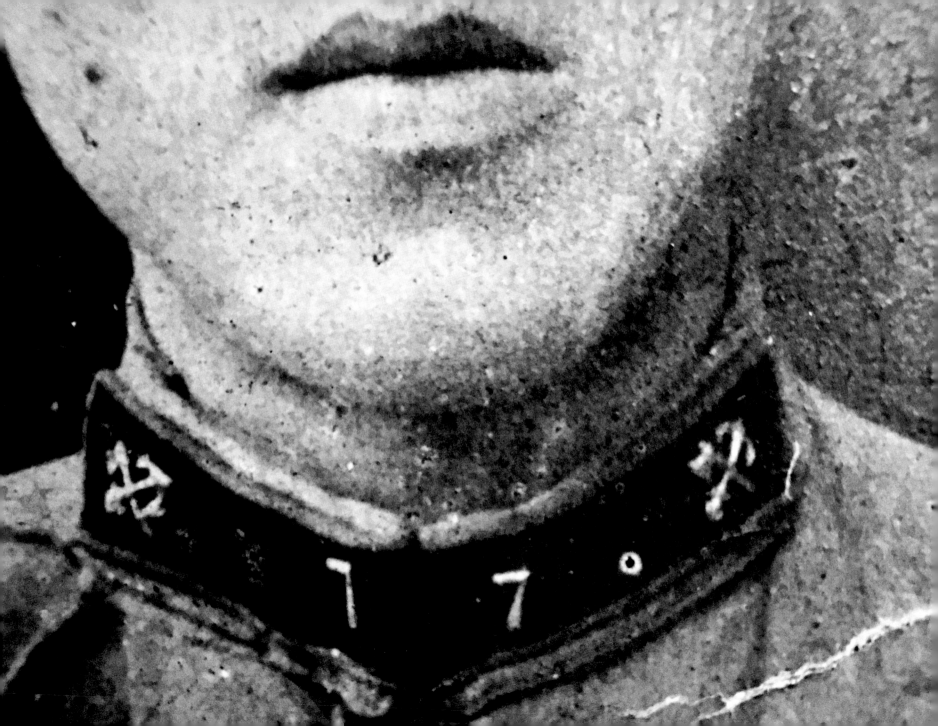

ЫБАКИ, РАБЫ

ЕМЛЯ НАША,

ЫЛИ УБИТЫ Н

PERM-36

PART TWO

The Last Camp

The Gulag is nowhere. It *was* everywhere. The word is an acronym for *glavnoye upravleniye lagerey*—The Head Directorate of Camps, a bureaucracy so sprawling that Alexander Solzhenitsyn likened it to an archipelago. The Gulag was formed in 1930 in order to put incarcerated Soviet citizens to work. Throughout the 1920s, the number of inmates had fluctuated. On the one hand, the Bolshevik regime strove to isolate its political opponents—it was Soviet Russia that pioneered the idea and the institution of the concentration camp—but on the other hand, the struggling economy could not afford to keep hundreds of thousands behind bars. In the late 1920s, the state experimented with forced labor without incarceration: even convicted murderers often received this kind of penalty. Still, by 1928 the number of inmates was growing inexorably. The state's repressive machine was getting stronger: In building a totalitarian system, the need to institute terror overpowered all other considerations, including economic ones. A radical solution was found in creating an entire separate economy of incarceration. The inmates would not simply be put to work in an effort to make the camp self-sustaining, as had been done in the 1920s, but the camps would exist to provide low-cost labor to the state. This was the Gulag.[xvi]

The Gulag was not an efficient system. In its early years, it was unable to create work for most of the inmates. But the terror machine was gaining speed, shoveling more and more people into the camps. Even though the death rate was extremely high—in 1933 as many as 15 percent of the inmates died of starvation, hypothermia, and disease—and even though the number of executions multiplied—in the Great Terror of 1937–1938 the state executed 681,692, more than ten times as many as in the preceding sixteen years combined—the population of the camps continued to grow. By 1938 it had topped two million. For the next quarter century, the total number of Gulag inmates fluctuated, but by the time Stalin died in 1953, approximately two and a half million people were being held in the camps.[xvii]

The Gulag was not a single entity—there were dozens of them: the Gulag of Timber Production, the Gulag of Railroad Construction, and the like. The Gulags contained camp directorates, which in turn contained multiple *lagpunkts*—"camp units"—the individual camps that made up the archipelago. But the camp itself was a vanishing act: It was created for a specific task—a construction project, a dig, a mine—and when the job was completed, when the tower was built, when the canal was dug, when the mine was depleted, when the forest was decimated—the camp disappeared, often without a trace. The riverside park in front of the hotel in the nuclear-science town of Dubna, outside of Moscow; the twenty-second floor of the main building of Moscow State University; the playground in front of the House of Culture in the village of Ust'-Omchug in the Far Eastern region of Kolyma—only a few surviving eyewitnesses knew that a *lagpunkt* had been there. The eyewitnesses rarely talked, and their memory died with them. The paperwork that documented a camp's existence was usually secret. When researchers finally gained access to it, it proved confusing. Camps often moved, taking their names with them. Two mines, hundreds of kilometers apart, would have the same name, that of the camp whose inmates had worked there. If the Bolshevik leader for whom the camp was named fell out of favor, the camp was renamed, confusing the record further. Just as the inmates were not individuals with names but, in the eyes of the regime, an undifferentiated mass with a job, so were the places they temporarily inhabited not places but functions.

It was often up to the inmates themselves to construct shelter out of whatever material was available. Unless timber was not to be found or the nature of the camp's project dictated otherwise, the barracks were rickety wooden structures that crumpled a couple of years after being abandoned. The wood rotted and melded into the landscape; only the barbed wire remained, though once its own wooden supports collapsed, it would fall on the ground, laying a trap for animals, hunters, and mushroom gatherers.

One camp lasted. In the Urals, a few hours outside the nearest large city of Molotov (named for Stalin's foreign minister who brokered the non-aggression pact that enabled the USSR and Nazi Germany to carve up Europe), a camp was built in 1946 to process lumber. Most of the inmates were not what was then called "politicals": They had not been tried for treason or espionage. Their infractions, whether real or imagined, were what the regime considered to be economic crimes against the state. They had been convicted of theft, fraud, or small-scale embezzlement. Their sentences were shorter than those of the politicals, and when Stalin died in 1953, they were amnestied—unlike the politicals, many of whom had to wait another three to five years. Many of the camps emptied out then and were abandoned to rot. This camp, however, was repurposed to house former secret-police officers: As Khrushchev consolidated power, he cleaned the ranks of the security apparatus. The camp was improved to suit the officers' needs, reduced as they were behind bars. Toilets were added to the barracks, along with low basins for foot-washing; the earlier generation of inmates had had the use of only two sinks per 125 inmates and had relieved themselves outside. The grounds were also improved.

96 The camp planted linden trees, which formed a grand alley that ran alongside the barracks.

In 1972, under Brezhnev, a specialized prison colony for law-enforcement officers was built elsewhere in the Urals and the camp was repurposed again. It became one of a dozen and a half places of incarceration—prison colonies, prisons, jails, and psychiatric institutions—used to house the "politicals" of the late Soviet period: human rights activists, pro-independence activists from the constituent republics of the USSR, religious-freedom activists, and underground writers and publishers. In addition, the camp now held men who had been convicted of being wartime Nazi collaborators. All of them were arrested and tried twenty-five years or more after the war ended; some had indeed assisted the German occupants actively or passively, while others had simply been caught up in the Soviet punitive machine. In the camp's new incarnation, the indoor toilets were eliminated in favor of new wooden outhouses. Some of the "politicals" were repeat offenders, which made them especially dangerous to the state. They served their time in the Special Zone, a prison within the camp where inmates were confined to cells that allowed in almost no natural light.

The nearest big city to the camp was no longer called Molotov—it had been restored to its pre-revolutionary name, Perm. Accordingly, the camp was now called Perm-36. Nearby prison colonies had the names Perm-35 and Perm-37; Perm itself was a four-hour drive away. In February 1988 several hundred inmates were released from the "political" prisons of the USSR under an amnesty that aimed to end the incarceration of the differently minded. Perm-36 was finally abandoned, left to rot.

In 1992 a Perm historian named Victor Shmyrov happened upon the remains of Perm-36.

"I was blown away," he told me twenty-four years later. "I'd been to many colonies, but this was something else. It was archaic. I knew right away that this was left over from the Gulag," by which he meant the Stalin era. Shmyrov decided to preserve the camp. He and his wife Tatyana Kursina, also a historian, organized security at the site to keep out looters—not that there was much to loot. In 1994, Shmyrov and Kursina started restoring the camp, patching up roofs, righting watchtowers that had fallen over. They put together a team of men from the local village and learned Soviet-era building trades, down to the art of straightening out old nails in order to reuse them. In 1995 Shmyrov quit his professorship and bought a chainsaw. They restored the camp's sawmill. The team of locals cut down trees in the surrounding woods; some of the wood went to the restoration project and the rest was sold to fund continuing labor. It took them twenty years to restore all twelve of the structures that made up Perm-36, including dormitory barracks, the solitary-confinement building, the sawmill, the guards' houses, the bathhouse, and the infirmary.

In 2005, Shmyrov and Kursina organized a festival for singer songwriters. The genre had been popular in the Soviet underground, so it seemed appropriate. They called it the Sawmill. It turned into an annual event, and an odd one: part NGO congress, part political-prisoner reunion, part rock concert, part curiosity. By the 2010s, it was drawing as many as fifteen thousand people, who set up camp in the surrounding fields and forests—Shmyrov had bought the land, which was cheaper than dirt. Volunteers led short tours of the camp itself, which, during the course of the festival, seemed to become something of a Gulag theme park.

In 2011 the regional governor, who harbored the unusual ambition of securing for Perm the title of a European Cultural Capital, offered Shmyrov and his team the resources and status to turn Perm-36 into a museum. Shmyrov and Kursina created several exhibition halls in the camp and contracted with an American museum-design firm for a full-scale contemporary interactive exhibit. Though for Shmyrov, the museum project was secondary: His mission was preservation. When Roginsky, the head of the Memorial Society in Moscow and a former political prisoner, told Shmyrov that the restored Perm-36 felt exactly like a real Soviet-era prison camp, Shmyrov accepted it as the ultimate compliment.

Sergei Kovaliov

What *did* Perm-36 feel like to an inmate? I asked Sergei Kovaliov, who spent five years there, starting in 1975. He was forty-five when he arrived—an old man by camp measure and by Soviet standards. He overheard two guards talking to each other.

"Why did they put the old guy in here? He seems harmless."

"He shouldn't have maligned the Soviet authorities."

Kovaliov's anti-Soviet activities, as these things were called, dated back to the 1950s, when, as a young biology Ph.D., he tried to speak up in defense of genetics, a banned science in the Soviet Union. In 1969, he co-founded the first independent human rights organization in the country. In 1971 he co-founded the *Chronicles of Current Events,* a typewritten underground newsletter that documented human rights abuses. He was arrested in 1974, convicted of "anti-Soviet agitation and propaganda," and sentenced to seven years in a prison camp and three years of internal exile.

His work on the *Chronicles* had prepared Kovaliov for Perm-36 pretty well: He knew many of the camp rules and the possible penalties for violations. What he did not know was how enforcement worked. Back when he was typing up news items for the *Chronicles*—often these were about an imprisoned dissident being placed in solitary as punishment for having been unshaven or for having failed to button his prison robe all the way to the top, or having worn his indoor slippers out on the porch, or having tea with a friend in another dormitory—he had sometimes found himself wondering how hard it can be to observe clearly articulated rules, however absurd, and what the point of violating them was, considering the cost. At Perm-36 he found out that no one usually observed most of the tiny nitpicky rules—and the guards paid no attention unless they needed a pretext for placing you in solitary. Then you could be busted, as Kovaliov once was, for having the top button of your robe undone while in the bedroom in the barracks. The whole point of having detailed, excessive rules was to guarantee the option of selective enforcement: If the rules had been applied evenly and consistently, they would not have been very useful as an instrument of control.

Penalties came in two varieties. There was solitary, and there was "confinement to a cell." Both kinds were administered in a single building a short walk from the dorms. "Confinement to a cell" was a bit easier to take—you got a mattress and a sheet, and you were fed every day. In solitary, food came every other day. That was harder than being on a hunger strike. When you don't eat at all, you don't feel hungry, but when you are fed every other day, you are starving most of the time. Solitary, on the other hand, was a short-term penalty, while confinement to a cell could last months. Kovaliov did two six-month stints of confinement to a cell, and he lost count of how many times he was placed in solitary.

Right around the time he lost track of his stays in solitary, he was summoned to the administration building—known grandly as "the headquarters"—and informed that he was incorrigible. This meant confinement to a cell. On his second day in his cell, Kovaliov received a visit from a young, rosy-cheeked captain.

"You probably want to know why you've been confined," said the captain.

"Actually, I had an entire protocol read to me," said Kovaliov. The protocol contained a litany of his nuisance infractions.

"That's all nonsense," said the captain and produced a piece of paper covered in fine, beady script. This was a draft of a letter a group of Perm-36 inmates had sent to a meeting of the Commission on Security and Cooperation in Europe, the first such meeting to

follow the signing of the Helsinki Accords, in which the Soviet Union had accepted a set of human rights obligations in exchange for trade concessions from the West. The letter said, in part:

We realize that the issue of political prisoners is not the top priority in today's world, and yet we dare to insist on advancing it, for it goes to the root of a most dangerous epidemic of our century: the tendency of a state to violate its own laws and declarations, using force in violation of both law and morality.

The Helsinki Accords, signed in 1975, contained four parts, which the drafters had called "baskets." The third of these baskets contained the human rights provisions on which Soviet dissidents could now base their calls for action. The letter continued:

We bear witness to the fact that even after the signing of the Helsinki Accords persecution for dissenting thought continues to be the regime's main preoccupation. We believe that the West understands, as we do, that the "third basket" is like air and daylight, without which all else loses meaning....We also hope that people of authority in the West understand that when they choose to seek compromise with forces of militant lawlessness...they accept the responsibility for eroding the ground on which we all stand.[xviii]

Kovaliov read the piece of paper the captain had handed to him, taking his time to demonstrate that he was seeing it for the first time.

"An excellent piece of writing," said Kovaliov. "I'd sign this myself."

"You did," said the captain.

100

Kovaliov learned three things from this conversation. One, that the inmate who worked the coal stove in the camp's heating plant, a Russian nationalist activist widely suspected of being a snitch, was more than a snitch: He had apparently tracked down and managed to extract this draft of the letter from a piece of pipe in the heating room in which the writers had cemented it. Kovaliov was sad to lose the draft, but grateful for the second thing he learned. The letter had apparently reached the addressee, because the captain knew that Kovaliov had signed it. The draft was unsigned, but the version of the letter that had been smuggled out had Kovaliov's signature first in a list of fourteen inmates.[1]

Kovaliov had smuggled this letter out himself. The inmates called the process "camp post." It utilized very thin paper—the inmates had once found an entire roll of electrical insulation paper, which was perfect for the task—and the thinnest possible ballpoint pen. The letter was written in handwriting as fine as one could master and then rolled up tightly and wrapped in plastic harvested from a clear plastic bag. Tie it up tightly with thread, use a match to melt and seal the ends, and then add another layer of plastic—they called it a "shirt"—and another and so on for a total of five. Then swallow. Then wait for your conjugal visit. There was no telling exactly when the visit would occur—inmates knew when they were eligible for their biannual visit, but the exact timing was up to the administration. One might wait for a few days or a few weeks. One tried to eat as little as possible while waiting, to keep the number

of bowel movements to a minimum. If it happened, though, one removed the outer "shirt" and swallowed the letter again. The conjugal visit, when it came, lasted three days. There would be plenty of eating then: Kovaliov's wife would have carried bags of groceries on the train from Moscow and then the bus from Perm. At some point, she would swallow the letter, which she would smuggle out of the camp in her own intestines, undetectable to the guard who searched her in the gynecological chair on the way out, as she had on the way in. The third thing that Kovaliov learned from his conversation with the young captain was that this was why he was here, in cell confinement.

He had spent many nights in this building before, in short-term solitary confinement. For that, you were brought in wearing only your underthings and slippers. There was no mattress on the wooden bunk. What you did was put your slippers on the bunk in place of a pillow and go to sleep. An hour, maybe an hour and a half later you would be woken up by the shivering of your own body. You jumped up, did jumping jacks and squats, and when you were exhausted, you crouched with your back against the lone heating pipe in the cell—its tiny diameter ensured that the space could never be heated, and the pipe itself, most nights, was just barely warmer than your body. If you rubbed your back against it, though, after a while you were warm enough to return to the bunk. You placed your head on your slippers again and were out like a light. An hour later your own shivering body would awaken you again.

---

[1] Kovaliov may have been mistaken in the assumption that the letter reached the Belgrade meeting: The transcripts of the conference do not contain the letter, though they do contain many similar documents (*Basket III: Implementation of the Helsinki Accords* (Washington: U.S. Government Printing Office, 1977), archived at https://www.documentcloud.org/documents/402803-17-basket-iii-helsinki-accords-hearings-volume-iv.html, accessed February 4, 2017). Excerpts from the letter used here were published in the *Chronicles of Current Events*.

Regulations guaranteed inmates the right to document the temperature in their cell—by law it had to be no lower than 14 degrees Celcius (57 Fahrenheit) in solitary. The guards supplied a thermometer on demand. The thermometer in solitary always showed 14 Celcius, even when the corners of the cell sparkled incongruously white because the dampness had frozen solid.

Being cold was a definitive experience of the camp. It was winter when Kovaliov was first brought there, a particularly brutal one with temperatures of minus-40 (the point where Fahrenheit and Celcius meet) and below. His first dorm was Barracks Number One, where the walls were part wood and part rags, which inmates used to stuff in the gaps between logs. If you took a rag out—usually in order to try to stuff it back in more tightly—the gap that opened up, about two inches wide, provided a clear view of the camp grounds. The thermometer in the dorm truthfully reported the temperature as ranging between 6 and 7 Celcius (43–45 Fahrenheit). Kovaliov started noting down the temperature at fixed times twice a day.

"I see you are incorrigible," a guard said when he noticed Kovaliov tracking the temperature. "You are continuing with your defamation."

"Defamation of the Soviet authorities" was law-enforcement vernacular for the crime of "anti-Soviet agitation and propaganda," for which Kovaliov had been sentenced.

"Whatever do you mean, sir?" Kovaliov responded. "Here is what the thermometer says, and here is what I wrote down—why would you call this defamation?"

Most of the time, though, in the dead of winter the guards stayed off the inmates' backs. They turned a blind eye to the fact that the inmates wore their cotton-stuffed robes and felt boots to bed. Not that these kept them warm: It was impossible to be still and stay warm. When inmates were awake, they continuously moved around the dorm. They conducted all their conversations as they paced up and down the length and breadth of the barracks.

It wasn't the guards' humanity that surprised Kovaliov. Like many dissidents, he held to an abiding belief in the goodness of human nature. He had assumed that the guards in the camps were cogs in the repressive machine, men who could have been decent if their jobs were less punishing. It was their sadism that surprised Kovaliov—this was the second thing that working on *Chronicles* had not prepared him for.

"You'd be behind the barracks, gathering mushrooms or picking watercress and one of the guards would come over and start humiliating you," Kovaliov told me. "He wouldn't reprimand you, he would just take pleasure in telling you, say, that you were turning into a sheep."

Kovaliov was talking to me in his Moscow apartment. After he was released from the camps in 1982, he spent three years in internal exile in the Kolyma Region in the Far East. He returned to Moscow in time for perestroika and became a public political activist. In 1994 President Yeltsin appointed him his human rights ombudsman, a job Kovaliov soon lost for his harsh criticism of the war in Chechnya. He served three terms in the Russian parliament before becoming, under Putin, once again a dissident. It was as a dissident that he attended all of Shmyrov's Sawmill festivals.

So how did it feel to be transported back into the space where his body and his spirit had suffered such abuse?

"Wonderful!" he exclaimed.

102   He saw my incredulous expression and explained: "You were just there at the wrong time of year."

I had visited Perm-36 in April, when the snow had melted into large, deep puddles that stood perfectly still, the same dense shade of gray as the low sky.

"You should see it in the summer. Some evenings there—the light is special, and the air—sometimes you'd be going behind the outhouse, because inside it was rather unpleasant and inconvenient and you avoided it if you could, so there you'd be, taking a piss behind the outhouse, and the air was like you could touch it, and the smell of those linden trees, and the sound of the birds singing."

Memory-Building

There is no reason Kovaliov's, or anyone else's, experience in the camps should make any more sense than the entire country's experience of state terror. Kovaliov earned his right to feel any way he wanted on a visit back to Perm-36—including, if he so wished, feeling "wonderful." But should the thousands of other visitors to the Sawmill Festival also feel wonderful about inhabiting the space of the last remaining Gulag camp?

Contemporary museums are concerned, perhaps more than anything else, with creating a mood. Yad Vashem, arguably the world's greatest museum devoted to historical tragedy, greets visitors with an explanation of its unusual architecture and its express purpose: to create the sense of space closing in, to give the guest a taste of losing hope. The Holocaust Memorial and the Jewish Museum in Berlin, among others, have followed a similar architectural-emotional strategy. When Shmyrov and Kursina were restoring Perm-36, they lacked the critical distance to even consider the question of mood. For them, authenticity of the physical objects was the beginning and the end of the conversation. The American-designed museum, had it been built as intended, would have preserved that authenticity while creating the physical and emotional distance for interpretation. But by then things had changed.

Shmyrov's 1992 impulse to restore Perm-36 harked to a perestroika-era fascination. As a child growing up in the region in the 1950s, he had heard of the camps and once followed a group of older boys to a secret place where they used torches to illuminate fallen watchtowers and coils of barbed wire. Whatever that was—it would be years before Shmyrov heard the word "Gulag"—he found the sight terrifying. He was too young and living in a place too remote to be aware of any of the Khrushchev-era revelations. When the

104 Thaw ended in 1964, Shmyrov was eighteen, a fresh conscript to the army. It was in the late 1980s that he read *The Gulag Archipelago* and the newspaper and magazine articles about the Great Terror. When he encountered Perm-36, he saw the embodiment of all these articles—actual, physical evidence that all he had read was true.

In the 1990s, while Shmyrov and Kursina worked on their restoration project and their interest in the history of the Gulag turned into an obsession, in the rest of the country it waned. Other Russians were much more concerned with making ends meet than with what their parents or grandparents had done decades ago, or even what had been done to them. In 2000, the tide turned altogether. Putin, Russia's new leader, was a former KGB officer deeply devoted to the Soviet-era mythology of the secret police. The new signals from the Kremlin, both spoken and tacit, were clear: The Soviet past would be recast in a nostalgic light. Stalin was now portrayed as a great leader who had won the Second World War and transformed the country into a great power. He might have gone overboard at times, it was acknowledged, but efforts to study these "excesses," as they were called, now drew suspicion and resentment—as though it had been the revelations of the perestroika era that had brought down the Soviet Union, the collapse of which Putin now called "the greatest geopolitical catastrophe of our time."

By the late aughts, Russian publishers were putting out dozens of popular titles of revisionist history: glorious biographies of Stalin and his henchmen, novels and imaginatively sourced nonfiction about the heroism of the secret police. Demand for the books was so high that many bookstores had entire sections devoted to them and some airport print vendors sold nothing but these titles. At the Sawmill Festival, an increasing number of visitors came wearing Stalin-era secret-police uniforms—there was now a shop in Moscow that specialized in making these to order. Some tents displayed portraits of Lavrentiy Beria, Stalin's last and most notorious secret-police chief. For the new Stalinists, Shmyrov's restored Gulag was becoming a pilgrimage site. Shmyrov and Kursina strove to engage these visitors in polite debate. On their turf, they still felt like they had the power and majority support.

A new political thaw began in 2008, when Putin temporarily gave the president's chair to Dmitry Medvedev, an unremarkable young lawyer who was desperately courting favor with the intelligentsia. He even promised to decree the formation of a national museum of Stalinist terror—though he shied from using the word "terror," falling back on "repressions." This was when Perm's ambitious governor offered up funding for a full-scale museum at Perm-36.

But Medvedev's museum decree never materialized. In 2012, Putin returned to the presidency and began a political crackdown. The Perm governor lost his job and left the country under duress. In 2013, authorities canceled the Sawmill Festival. Then they took over Perm-36. Shmyrov, Kursina, and their board, which included Kovaliov, tried to fight the takeover by going to court and by pulling strings wherever they could find them. Shmyrov and Kursina lost their jobs and the project on which they had worked for nearly a quarter of a century. News spread that the country's only Gulag museum situated in an actual camp was now becoming a museum of the Gulag, one that glorified the camps by showing the environment in them to be carefree and their mission to be noble.

By this time, many museums of Soviet terror had been built— outside of Russia. One could travel from Riga to Warsaw, Berlin,

Budapest, and other cities and visit such a museum in each of these capitals (I have). Each museum tells a story. The one in Riga guides the visitor through a Soviet police jail. Warsaw built a museum of betrayal—when, in the fall of 1944, Soviet troops stood by as Nazi troops massacred the people of the city, to make it that much easier for Soviet occupation to take hold once they left. Berlin has several museums of the surveilled life. Budapest's House of Terror tells the stories of the Nazi and Soviet occupations side by side, along the way conveniently eliding Hungary's history of collaboration with Nazi Germany. But such is the nature of these and other history museums: They assert the basic goodness of a nation. The story they tell of Soviet terror is, first and foremost, the story of a hostile power, an Other who perpetrated the atrocities. It is also a story of hope: Now that the occupation is over, these countries are free to be their good selves. But what story is a Russian museum of state terror supposed to tell?

For seventy years, Russians exerted the force of state terror against themselves. The country was not occupied by a hostile power. Nor was the terror exercised against any population perceived as different. The millions who died anonymously in the Gulag were not necessarily members of ethnic or religious minorities, or even homosexuals: The population of the camps largely corresponded to the population of the country, which meant that the majority of inmates were ethnic Russians who had led regular lives until they were randomly assigned the title of "enemy of the people." Russians had no other nation to blame for their nightmare. Nor could they construct a narrative of a short bout of national insanity, which is one of the stories contemporary Germans tell about their twelve years of Nazism. The Soviet regime lasted seven

decades. Russians could not even divide themselves and their ancestors into neat categories of victim, perpetrator, and bystander, as the Germans had done. In Russia, most people had played the roles of both victim and perpetrator. There were no bystanders.

Every museum, indeed every country, ultimately aims to tell a story about the goodness of its people. If the blame for Russia's dark twentieth-century past could not be displaced onto someone else or even onto a discrete group of Russians, the remaining option would be to transform the story of darkness into a story of glory. In this narrative, Stalin would be a fearless leader who saved the world from the Nazi scourge. He might have overstepped at times—people may have suffered or even died needlessly—but in the end he would go down in history as the savior of the free world, and he and the country he led would thereby be absolved of their crimes. It helped that most of the deaths had been anonymous and the crimes could be abstracted. As for the ones that had been documented—humanized—by family members and Memorial Societies, these could be trivialized: To make an omelet, you have to break some eggs.

This was what I expected to see when I visited the revamped Perm-36 museum in April 2016. I thought it would tell me that the Soviet regime—and the Gulag administrations by extension—had been heroic, and its wrongs, if there were any, had been negligible. But what I saw was something else altogether.

"Here you can see a typical camp barracks. Construction dates to 1946." The tour guide is a former village schoolteacher in her thirties. She sounds very official, very much like the tour guides from every mind-numbing museum visit from my childhood. She leads us to a former dormitory barracks that has some information displays on the walls. The first few contain pictures of former Perm-36 inmates.

"Sergei Adamovich Kovaliov, an outstanding geneticist, was an inmate here." She sounds proud. A few days later I will hear the exact same pride in the words of an expert witness at the trial of a protest artist in Moscow: The expert witness will claim that the KGB headquarters in Moscow (which the artist is accused of vandalizing) is an "object of cultural significance" because many great Russian artists and writers had been confined in its cellar. This is a new expression of the conflation of victims and perpetrators particular to the history of Soviet terror—where the state claims credit for the talents and accomplishments of its victims, as though by interning, torturing, or executing the people it has absorbed their gifts and made them its own.

The tour guide leads us around the dormitory at a sprinter's pace. I ask to be left to wander and look around the barracks.

"Not allowed," she says.

"Why not?"

"You have to have an escort with you at all times."

"Why is that?"

"Because it's a museum."

This takes me back to my Soviet childhood, when it sometimes seemed that every single word was used to mean its opposite. You would think that a museum is precisely the sort of place where people would wander and look around.

We look at the camp's security setup, a nine-layer system of barbed wire, electrified wire, fine mesh wire designed to envelop and entrap a person, a strip of sand, a line of floodlights, a wall.

"Some people tried to escape early on," says the tour guide. "But there isn't a town for hundreds of kilometers, and there is only one road—no one got far. And then they built this, and there were no more escape attempts." She sounds proud again. She seems to take pride in everything that works. Her feeling is unencumbered by ideas of good and evil.

We return to the barracks, where another room houses an exhibit called "The Evolution of the Bed." It shows a progression from two-tier wooden bunks to single-tier ones, to proper narrow beds with metal headboards and footboards. As the Gulag matured, the exhibit shows, its inmates slept in increasing comfort.

A quote in stylized white-on-black cursive adorns the back wall. It's pulled from a story by Varlam Shalamov, a writer who spent more than fifteen years in the Gulag, a couple of them in the Perm Region and the rest in Kolyma. He managed to write about the camps in a way that avoided the traps of sense-making and redemptive narrative: His short stories place the reader inside the camps and refuse to zoom out. The quote is, "Man is lucky to have the ability to forget. Memory is always ready to let go of the bad and hold on only to the good."

Is this a joke? The quote is from one of Shalamov's Kolyma stories. Here is the context:

Friendship takes its root neither in need nor in hardship. Life's difficulties that the fairy tales of fiction tell us are a necessary condition of forging friendship are simply not difficult enough. If need and hardship have brought people together, have created the bonds of friendship, that means simply that the need was not that great and the hardship was not that extreme. If grief can be shared with friends, then this grief is not that deep or that acute. Real need exposes only one's own inner strength and bodily might, determines the limits of only one's own ability, physical endurance, and moral fortitude.

We all knew that if any of us survived, it would be by accident. Funny thing: When I was young, I used to have a saying that I applied to all my mishaps and failures: "At least I won't starve to death." I was certain, with my entire physical being, of the truth of this phrase. And then at the age of thirty I became a man who was actually dying of hunger, who was literally physically fighting for a single slice of bread—and that was long before the war came.

When the four of us found ourselves at the Duskanye Creek, we knew that we had not been brought together to become friends: we knew that if we survived we would hardly want to see one another. We would not want to recall the bad: being driven mad by hunger, using our dinner pots to try to boil our clothes to get the lice out, the endless lying by the fire, lying-fantasizing, telling tall tales about food, fighting with one another, and dreaming identical dreams, for all of us had the same dream over and over: loaves of rye bread flying past us like airplanes, or like angels.

Man is lucky to have the ability to forget. Memory is always ready to let go of the bad and hold on only to the good. There was nothing good at Duskanye Creek, nor had there been anything good ahead, nor had there been anything good in the paths that had brought us there. The North had poisoned us for life, and we knew this. Three of us had given up on life, and only Ivan Ivanovich continued to toil with the same tragic force as before.[xix]

Shalamov was describing a time when he was near death in the camps in Kolyma. But I don't think this is a joke. I suspect someone

was given the assignment of finding a Shalamov quote to use in the exhibit—Shalamov being the most famous writer to have served time in these parts—and that someone probably googled "famous Shalamov quotes" and found this one, among a dozen others, for the line about memory had been found catchy by others and had made it onto some internet lists, and then someone probably picked it because it sounded positive.

Later that evening when I see Shmyrov and Kursina again, Kursina will rail against the "Evolution of the Bed" exhibit, which she has heard contains contemporary, multicolored wool blankets. She is right: The exhibit violates their rules of authenticity. Kovaliov will tell me that the blankets in the dorms were the thin gray variety. "But," he will note with a scientist's precision and a dissident's honesty, "they were warm." Roginsky will acknowledge that conditions in which inmates were kept did improve from decade to decade. He himself had it much better than Shalamov.

The problem with the exhibit is not inaccuracy or inauthenticity. Nor does it glorify the Gulag, as people have claimed. The problem is cacophony. How is one to understand a story that tells one, in essence, that great people spent time here, that conditions were bad but got better, that it's a good thing that they couldn't escape, and that the ability to forget is a blessing? There is no story here, and there certainly isn't a mood, with the tour guide chattering incessantly: "And if you ask me about games [I did not], playing cards were forbidden and there was one chess set per fifty people."

The cacophony creates a sense of moral neutrality. There is no story—of an occupation, an Other, a mistake—because there can be no such story. But what is history without a story? This is the intolerable contradiction inherent in the work Shmyrov and

Kursina and hundreds of others tried to take on. They documented terror, which is random—nonsensical—by definition. Flige and Iofe in St. Petersburg, Roginsky in Moscow, and the cultural historian Etkind warned against the temptation of sense-making, and tried to avoid it at all cost in their own work. The terror was senseless. But was it also meaningless? They would argue that it was not—in the sense that it must be known and remembered. But known and remembered how?

Back in the 1990s, Kovaliov argued for a sort of nationwide repentance. Since everyone was both a victim and a perpetrator, or the descendant of both victims and perpetrators, then everyone deserved an apology and everyone had to make one. In Kovaliov's world, populated by people who had been willing to go to jail for their convictions, this seemed an unproblematic proposition. He volunteered to be the first to apologize—and he tried to, on a few public occasions, back in the day when he was a nationally prominent political leader. But his proposal confused most Russians. What did they have to apologize for? Why was it they who had to apologize? They had never imprisoned, tortured, or executed anyone. Why should they offer to share the responsibility for events that an increasing number of their compatriots don't even view as crimes?

The world offers no models for this kind of predicament. The closest, on the face of it, may be the developed nations, such as Australia and Canada, that have apologized for their treatment of indigenous populations. On the face of it, these are nation states saying "sorry" to their own people. But on closer examination, it is post-colonial powers apologizing for the crimes of colonization, addressing people whom the governments still view as Other. Has any country actually apologized to all of its people, in the name of all of its people? It may be too much to ask.

The cacophony conveys the sense that the Gulag meant everything and nothing. That is the distinguishing characteristic of the Putin-era historiography of Soviet terror. It says, in effect, that it just happened, whatever.

56.

f miitalumni ⊙ vipuskniki_miit B miit_museum ⊙ miit_museum www.miit.su #миит120л

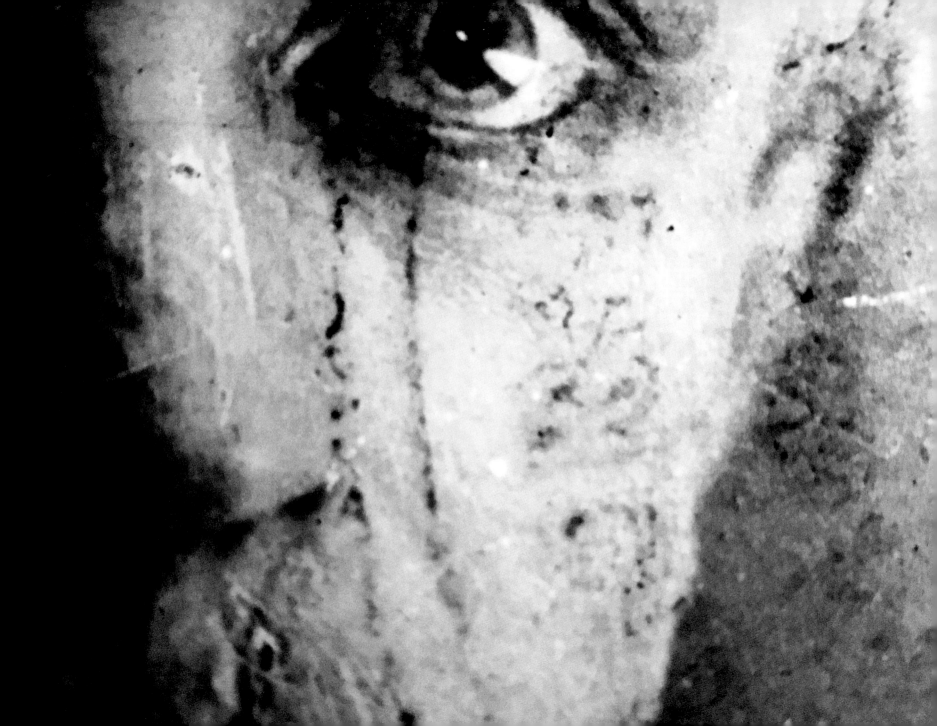

KOLYMA

PART THREE

Butugychag

If the Gulag was anywhere, it was in Kolyma. There were a dozen different camp directorates in the Far Eastern region of Russia, each of which held between two thousand and two hundred thousand inmates at any one time. Millions of people went through Kolyma camps over the course of twenty years, and estimates of the number who died range from hundreds of thousands to two million. They were delivered here by way of Vladivostok—itself at least a week's, more often several months' journey from central Russia. In Vladivostok the inmates were loaded onto ships for the journey to Magadan, the administrative center of the Kolyma region. The trip by sea lasted no less than nine days. A standard ration for this leg consisted of one herring and three glasses of water per person. Many died at sea. At least one vessel, with some twelve thousand inmates on board, was stranded in the ice floes; everyone on the ship died. When inmates did make it to Kolyma, they were often deposited in the woods, on the hills, in bear land, to mine the gold, tin, or uranium, and to build not only shelter for themselves but also the factories in which inmates would work long after the current crop had succumbed to cold, hunger, and disease. They also built the city of Magadan, the capital of this land of the Gulag. Most of those who came here never left, even if they lived to be released from the camps. It was as though they had been taken to an island with no right of return. Even after the Gulag had shut down, after the city of Magadan, modeled after the pseudo-Parisian architecture of St. Petersburg, had been completed, after the Soviet Union collapsed and people had long been traveling to Moscow by plane—an eight-hour flight—the mental habit persisted: Local residents still think of Kolyma as an island and refer to the rest of Russia as the mainland.

When the time came, or seemed to come, to memorialize the victims of the Gulag, Magadan seemed the obvious place to start.

Ernst Neizvestny, arguably the best-known Soviet-born sculptor on the planet, had an idea for a monument that would triangulate the Gulag. Neizvestny had once been an official Soviet monumentalist, a successful one. He had created sculptures memorializing the Second World War. During the Thaw, like many other Soviet artists, Neizvestny started experimenting with less-realistic and less-heroic—which is to say, less-Soviet—art. When Khrushchev saw Neizvestny's new scupltures at an officially sanctioned high-profile show in Moscow, he grew incensed. "Why do you distort the faces of Soviet people?" he railed. In a rambling, stream-of-consciousness speech Khrushchev called the art in the show "degenerative" and used the word "faggots" at least three times.[xx] Just like that, Neizvestny was transformed into an opponent of the regime. In the 1970s, he emigrated and settled in New York. When the Soviet Union collapsed, Neizvestny emerged as the clear candidate for creating a monument to the victims of Soviet terror. The need for such a monument also seemed self-evident. Neizvestny designed a monument called the Mask of Sorrow. He envisioned a giant face, deformed by tragedy, a version of which would be erected on hills overlooking three Russian cities: Magadan; the far northern city of Vorkuta; and Ekaterinburg, the largest city in the Urals. Local Memorial Societies took up the cause of creating a Mask of Sorrow in each of the three cities.

This was the time when Memorial Societies were forming all over the country. In the Kolyma region, history that had been buried in plain sight began to emerge. Memorial chapters appeared not only in Magadan but also in surrounding villages, which had once served as Gulag administrative centers. In Ust'-Omchug, about four hours north of Magadan, a geologist named Inna Gribanova started researching the camps. I met her when I traveled to Kolyma in the summer of 1999. She had lived here since 1968, when she got a coveted post-graduation job assignment to the Far East. All geologists wanted to be heroes, she explained: The losers were assigned to work subway digs while the winners were sent to prospect for gold thousands of miles from the capital. She said that she had "always known" that there had been labor camps around here but had not taken an active interest in the issue until the 1980s, when one of the national magazines published a former inmate's memoir about these parts. Specifically, it described a camp about an hour's drive from the village. It was called Butugychag, and word was—now that word had emerged—that this had been one of the biggest and almost certainly the deadliest of all the big and deadly camps around here. The inmates there had been used to mine tin and uranium.

There was talk of creating a museum at Butugychag. Gribanova was opposed. Why spend money on a place no one was ever going to visit: an eight-hour flight from Moscow followed by a five-hour drive and at least an hour's hike, weather permitting? She was concerned with something else: bones. She heard from people, and then went and saw for herself, that there were human bones strewn all over the former camp grounds. She assembled a group of high school students who volunteered to help her bury the remaining remains of the prisoners of Butugychag. They quickly realized why the bodies had never been properly buried: The ground was granite. A shovel could lift no more than a few inches of topsoil, which would be ripped off the body by the first strong gust of wind.

Around the same time, in 1989, the local authorities were alerted to the fact that background radiation levels were high at the old camp.

They tried to ban entry to everyone, especially Gribanova and her young volunteers. She argued back passionately in the local newspaper, stressing the need to preserve what was there. In one article she compared Butugychag to Buchenwald. She had just traveled abroad for the first time and had seen how the memory of Nazi concentration camps was preserved in East Germany. She found herself starting the local Ust'-Omchug chapter of the Memorial Society.

She lost her job—not because of her activism but because the state was no longer funding geological research in the area. All the geologists and most of the people who had worked for them left. Ust'-Omchug very nearly emptied out. One of the two schools closed, and the other couldn't fill its classes. The only people who stayed were those who had no place to go, many of them former inmates—and Gribanova, who found herself unable to abandon her memory project. She started a museum, first a room and then a couple of rooms in the local House of Culture.

In 1999, Gribanova took me to Butugychag. We rode in a vehicle designed for the Soviet armed forces: It was a bare and uncomfortable ride, but the vehicle's off-road qualities were unparalleled. Still, we had to disembark about a mile from our destination. The creek through which we were driving ran too deep from this point on. We walked along the water and then climbed up a hill. The hill was steep and covered with black rocks, as though a giant had sprinkled the rocks on the granite monolith underneath. Every step began with testing one's foothold. Gribanova, who was in her late fifties, sat down on a rock near the top of the hill, her hand on her chest, apparently attempting to calm her rapidly beating heart.

"How high have we climbed?"

"Not that high," she said. "About two hundred meters, four hundred maximum. One inmate memoir says the climb was a kilometer. But inmates tend to exaggerate."

We climbed that hill on a warm day in July, during the roughly two-week period locals think of as summer. The inmates, who subsisted on starvation rations, had climbed it year-round, when the rocks were covered in ice and the temperatures were often below minus-40. Gribanova had brought me up to the top in order to show me something unimaginable and indescribable: the adit of what had once been a tin mine. It was a cave roughly fifty yards in diameter. It narrowed gradually as we walked toward the frozen center of the rock.

"Maybe it's not right to call this an adit," said Gribanova. "It's more of a quarry. Created by the slaves of Rome in the middle of the twentieth century."

They had used dynamite to rip apart the rocks. The inmates then loaded the ore—rocks that weighed, on average, between a hundred and two hundred pounds—onto carts. Smaller chunks were known as "crumbs." The explosion often propelled "crumbs" out of the adit. It was the women's job to collect the "crumbs" and load them onto carts too. Gribanova had found the handwritten memoir of a geologist who had done an internship at the camp as a student in 1950. She quoted from memory:

They crawled up the hill like a bunch of giant ants. At the opening of the adit they were counted and allowed to enter one by one, like toothpaste being squeezed from a tube. Twelve hours later everything was repeated in reverse order: It took a long time to line them all up at the exit from the adit, and then they were counted. The count always came up short.

Sometimes they were held there for hours as the adit was searched—until the last blood-soaked robe had been extracted.

The robes were numbered, allowing the guards to use them for their reports. The bodies themselves could then be left in the adit.

By the time I met her, Gribanova had spent a decade looking for information on the camps. She collected press clippings, such as one from Magadan Pravda from 1949: An article said that Berlag, the Gulag subdivision of which Butugychag was a part, held fourteen thousand people, of whom 44.4 percent had been convicted of the crime of nationalism, 31.3 percent of having "anti-Soviet connections," 10.4 percent of belonging to anti-Soviet organizations, 9.8 percent of espionage, 3.7 percent of terrorism, and 0.4 percent of Trotskyism. The problem with an article like this was everything. Granted, none of the inmates had received a fair trial, if they received a trial at all; all or most were not in fact guilty of any of the acts for which they had been convicted. Just as likely, the statistics published in the paper were also false.

Soviet citizens learned about the Gulag from two different and often contradictory sources: from the media, which reported almost exclusively on show trials and political crimes, and from personal experience of seeing friends, family, or neighbors arrested, usually for no apparent reason. Beginning in the late 1980s, Moscow activists published some documents that had been classified. These included nationwide statistics and eventually added up to a comprehensive map of the Gulag. But these documents came in dribs and drabs and shed little light on what had happened here, in the heart of the Gulag, so far away from Moscow.

Gribanova's information was similar in nature—press clippings and personal stories—except there was a lot more of this information than most Russian citizens ever saw. At the same time, much of the information—the press clippings, the inmate memoirs, the personal stories passed from person to person was unreliable or just demonstrably false. Did accumulating more unreliable source material add up to more knowledge or less?

In an effort to gain a solid foothold on the information, Gribanova started writing out any Butugychag-related names whenever she came across them in the media. Over the course of ten years she created a stack of two hundred and four index cards.

Valentina Ivanovna Avanesova.
Arrested in 1947.
Sentence: five years.
After release, lived in Kulu.

A note in pencil: "Daughter works at the post office."

Many of those who survived the camps never left Kolyma. They had no money for the journey home, and often no home to return to. Many were simply not allowed to leave, some because their sentences included restrictions on future places of residence and others simply because their labor was still needed. Some years all inmates who made it to the end of their sentences were compelled to take jobs in the camps. They traded in their prison robes for camp-staff uniforms and moved to different barracks. They were now called *vol'nonayomniye*—a term that specifically described those who worked in the camps not as inmates but as hires. Their working conditions improved, sometimes marginally, and they received better food rations. In effect, what on paper looked like release was a promotion within the closed economy of the Gulag.

Gribanova had located sixteen former inmates in Ust'-Omchug. They lived in an area on the outskirts of the village—they had effectively squatted the land in the mid-1950s, building small Ukrainian-type houses in a tight, self-contained semi-circle. Most of the people who lived in this neighborhood after Butugychag had been Ukrainians sentenced for aiding the Germans during Nazi occupation.

I knocked on the door of the brightest-white of the houses: It's a Ukrainian custom to whitewash houses every year, adding bluing to the paint to make the house shine in the sun. A heavy woman answered the door. She told me that her name was Anna Dzenkiv and her prisoner number had been B-1-762. She was sixteen when the war began, twenty when it ended and she was arrested and shipped to Kolyma. Her crime was that she had cooked for the German officers who had moved into the family house during the occupation. She served nine years in Butugychag. When she was released in 1954, she was not allowed to return to Ukraine. Someone told her about the houses on the outskirts of Ust'-Omchug and she came here. She stayed in the house that now, in 1999, was hers. Back then it belonged to a Ukrainian man who had been released in 1950. Another inmate staying here was Ivan—he had been released a year earlier. Anna married him.

She worked as a janitor in Ust'-Omchug. After Khrushchev denounced Stalinist "repressions," Dzenkiv and her husband went to court. In 1962, they were allowed to return to Ukraine, and even to live in Dzenkiv's childhood home. She couldn't get used to life there, though. After two years, the couple returned to Kolyma.

She was seventy-four when I interviewed her. Her husband had died fifteen years earlier. Her son had been killed in a knife fight two years before that. She had a daughter who was living in Ukraine. I pushed for some expression of resentment or regret for a life that had been stolen. I got none.

"They needed people to work here," she told me. "You have to work all your life. That's Kolyma for you."

Inna Gribanova

I return to Ust'-Omchug in 2016—and Misha and I immediately get detained by the local police. After some haggling over the legality of our presence in the area, we are on our way to Butugychag. The vehicle we are riding in is Japanese, like most cars here these days; its off-road qualities are even better than those of the Soviet military vehicle. Our guide is Gribanova, now seventy-five years old and officially the director of the history exhibit of the Ust'-Omchug museum. This morning she woke up to find that her phone had been disconnected and she was required to report to the police—all this because the police had apparently learned that we were on our way to Ust'-Omchug.

The car is better, but the road is worse. The creek, which swells each year with melted snow from the hills, has overflowed a couple of times since I was last here, and this has transformed the landscape. The road, or what can be used as road, now ends much farther from the mines. The hike that follows has grown harder, too, and

Gribanova will no longer attempt to finish it. She walks with us for a while, then sits down on the remains of a stone wall. The stones are large—two to six times the size of a brick—and irregularly shaped, and laid on top of one another by hand. All Gulag structures in this area have walls put together in this manner. The uranium factory, where we stopped on the way here, had the same stone walls, but these had been plastered over. Now most of the plaster has chipped off, carpeting the floor and concealing objects only Gribanova's trained eye picks out: mittens, boots, large pans used in the giant ovens here. Gribanova has some theories about how the uranium factory functioned—a succession of crushing, soaking, and heating operations—but these are only educated guesses. The people who worked here didn't live to write memoirs.

The wall where Gribanova has stopped now appears to be a part of a construction project that was never completed. Years ago, after

146 the initial back-and-forth about walling off Butugychag or turning it into a museum subsided, Gribanova advocated for taking this single masonry fragment and moving it to the highway, many miles from here, to mark the turn-off toward the camp. Few people would turn, even fewer would be able to get anywhere near Butugychag itself, but at least those who drove by would know that something had happened here. Negotiations involved the local administration and the transportation authority, and they kept stalling until Gribanova gave up. Now she stops at the unfinished and abandoned wall to give us directions: Keep walking along this creek, which is called *Podumay*—"Think About It." We will have to cross three more creeks that come in from the hills to our right: the first one is called *Chort* (Devil), the second is *Bes* (Demon), and the third is *Shaytan* (Satan). Chort and Bes creeks had uranium mines in them. Shaytan led to tin. We are to veer right at Shaytan and walk along the creek. The adits will be up the hill to our left.

The terrain gets more difficult. There are no paths. We climb when that seems right and tread the narrow bank of the creek when it seems possible to avoid stepping in the water. On the side of a small hill, we suddenly come upon a Russian Orthodox cross. Barbed wire is wound around the top. At the base of the cross, there is a large rock with some smaller stones arranged on top of it. This is the first time I have seen this, a Jewish sign of memory, anywhere in Russia. A length of barbed wire is coiled next to the rock, in a way that looks intentional. There is also an old wooden box, a plank, and a couple of lengths of pipe. I cannot tell what was placed here by someone who was designing a monument and what was already here, an accident the designer couldn't or wouldn't correct. When we return and I tell Gribanova about the monument, she will be surprised—she has never seen it or heard of it. This memorial is the opposite of public art anywhere else—anonymous and unseen, it is not in fact public, because there is no one here to witness its existence.

We keep walking. The floods, rains, and mudslides have reshuffled the remains of the camp, restacking manmade structures and natural ones. We find ourselves on top of buildings, suddenly in the middle of what used to be buildings, and behind barbed wire. We are able to stick to the rocky edge of the creek for a while, until Podumay runs into Shaytan and it is time to turn upward. We climb, grabbing hold of branches to pull ourselves up where the branches aren't so dry that they would snap. Now I find myself facing a stone wall. I realize that I have, so far, avoided using any of the camp structures for physical support. Here, though, I have no choice but to cling to the wall as I move along a narrow ledge just below it, until I come to an opening—and immediately recognize the architecture of the building I have now entered. There is a corridor, subdivided by a grate, with metal doors on either side of the corridor leading to tiny dark rooms with walls of rock. The materials are different, but the layout and dimensions are exactly the same as in the super-high-security barracks for repeat political offenders at Perm-36.

And then, about fifty yards up the hill, there is the rocky foundation of what was probably a wooden structure. The small platform is entirely covered with shoes—old, well-worn and beaten down by weather. I have seen piles of shoes like this in Holocaust museums the world over, from Auschwitz to Yad Vashem to the Holocaust Museum in Washington, D.C. Piles of thousands of shoes have become a device for conveying the scale of the killing:

Each flattened useless pair once belonged to someone who walked the earth. Here, no one arranged the pile of shoes for the purpose of impressing the visitor. Butugychag has museumified itself, but no one will see its display.

We never made it to the adits or the camp graveyard that Gribanova used to try to look after. It may no longer be physically possible, at least at this time of year—in early June, when the entrances to the adits, visible from the bottom of the hill, are blocked by snowbanks. Perhaps we would have made it if we had had a guide—but no one left in this area knows this terrain well enough to guide us. When we return to the car at dusk, Gribanova and our driver, a software engineer from Magadan who makes extra money driving tourists—usually hunters—have made a fire by the creek. There is sweet tea from a kettle blackened by many fires, and food cooked by the driver's wife. We sit by the fire as the sun sets over the black hills.

"I see you don't like Putin so much," Gribanova suddenly says. The last time we saw each other was two weeks before Putin was yanked from obscurity to be appointed prime minister. Within months he began restoring the image of the secret police going all the way back to czarist Russia.

"I think the feeling is mutual," I joke, assuming that I am speaking to a like-minded person.

"I like him," Gribanova corrects me firmly.

I don't understand how this is possible.

"All my life I have been in the minority," she explains. "I grew tired of it. For once, I wanted to vote for the winner. And I did."

I can understand the desire to belong to the majority. But how does this square with the work of Gribanova's life? How can she support a president who has declared her organization, the Memorial Society, a "foreign agent"—the contemporary equivalent of an "enemy of the people"—and has led the whitewashing of Stalin's terror?

It turns out that Gribanova no longer considers herself part of Memorial. The local chapter has been shuttered, and her own views on the terror and the camps have gradually adjusted. She now believes that the figures published by Soviet officials in the late 1980s—the thousands of executions a day in 1937 and the millions that went through the Gulag—were politically expedient exaggerations. Nor does she believe that many, never mind most, of the inmates were innocent. The driver adds that the camps were necessary to prepare the country for the big war. This is an increasingly popular interpretation, which uses the central myth of Russian history—the Soviet victory in the Second World War, which transformed the country into a global superpower—to justify the terror that preceded the war. Gribanova agrees.

The following day at Gribanova's lovingly maintained museum, where seventeen years ago I heard a story of moral clarity and outrage, I will encounter a cacophony. The space is bigger now, and the exhibit is larger, but the story is mangled. There are charts and flags and maps. In a far corner there are binders with newspaper clippings from the late 1980s. I find the piece in which Gribanova referred to Buchenwald as an example for local memorialization efforts to follow.

"What do you think of this comparison now?" I ask. "Butugychag and Buchenwald—is it fair?"

"Yes," she says. "Of course not."

Then she walks quickly to the other end of the room and beckons me to come look at something else.

"I said, 'Let's get inside your mask. Make it into a solitary cell. We'll take the stuffing from an abandoned camp. Everyone will feel like an inmate for a minute.'"

Both Kazaev and Etlis have long since left Magadan, whose population is dwindling. (I interviewed Kazaev in Moscow.) I am taken to the Mask by Vera Sergeeva, Magadan's one-woman department of culture: She oversees the city's museums, monuments, and libraries. She unlocks the Mask with her key. We go through a door in the front of the monument—the face—and climb a narrow stairway to find ourselves in a replica of a solitary-confinement cell. A second tiny space is stuffed with objects that Sergeeva calls "tools of labor": a piece of rail, a pair of boots, an aluminum bowl, a wooden post with a rusted can lid nailed to it, with a number embossed in it crudely with a nail. These kinds of posts were used to mark graves, or what passed for graves. Gribanova once assumed that the numbers on the lids corresponded to inmate numbers, but she was wrong: they were the numbers used to keep track of the graves themselves—plot numbers, though there were no plots. The rest of the tin can would have been used to make a bowl or a pot for heating up food on a fire: the kind of aluminum bowl displayed here was a rare luxury in these camps.

"All the objects are genuine," says Sergeeva.

There is a robe, a pair of tall boots, a barrel, and another aluminum bowl, this one with a spoon.

Sergeeva leads me out of the room and onto a stairway leading down: we exit the mask through the back of the head. She locks the door.

"How do people usually get to go inside?" I ask.

"They don't," she says. "Unless it's an official visit on some big occasion. Like Russia Day or something."

She goes on to explain that no more than three or four people can fit inside at any one time, and the museum cannot be staffed because it cannot be heated—so it stays locked. This museum, in other words, is virtually secret.

From the outside, the Mask of Sorrow is overburdened, which renders it inscrutable. It is over sixty feet tall (this requires a twenty-foot foundation that reaches all the way through the permafrost and rests on the granite monolith). The front of the Mask is divided by a cross. In place of the right eye there is a bell. The left side of the mask disintegrates into more than a dozen smaller masks, which symbolize tears.

"To my mind, because it's the left side of the face that's split open and has all the little masks on it, this symbolizes memory," says Sergeeva. "Because memory resides in the left hemisphere."

Built into the back of the Mask are two anthropomorphic statues: a realistically sculpted woman on her knees and a man impaled on a cross.

"This is the Kolyma Crucifixion," says Sergeeva, as though the Kolyma crucifixion were a known term. "The cross, stakelike, pierces the body of the inmate and the strength the inmate is manifesting—at least I think he is manifesting—is strength not of the body but of the spirit."

Like many of the people I have met, Sergeeva has her own visions of an ideal monument to the victims of the Gulag. It is not the Mask of Sorrow. She says that the monument is a cage full of stones, each of which looks like a head. She has lobbied for it for years, unsuccessfully. She has seen the monument on the internet;

she tells me that it is located in the Sculpture Garden in Moscow. I don't think that she realizes that the beautiful-sounding Sculpture Garden is a repository of unwanted statues.

We leave the Mask of Sorrow and go to a museum—the apartment of Vadim Kozin, who was the city's most famous resident when he died here in 1994. Kozin was already the country's most famous performer of torch songs—possibly the Soviet Union's most famous singer, full-stop—when he arrived here half a century earlier.

We walk up to the fourth floor of a plain gray five-story apartment building. Sergeeva opens the door to a parlor suitable for a Liberace concert: a baby grand piano with a bench, both in red lacquer; a half-dozen blood-red plush velour benches and a few couches in clashing red are lined up for the audience. The floor is white lacquer, inlaid with replicas of Hollywood Boulevard stars.

Really? Was this how Kozin lived here in the 1980s and 1990s?

"Of course not," says Sergeeva. "It's all been redone. They didn't even have these kinds of building materials twenty years ago."

The piano, she told me, was Kozin's, except underneath the red lacquer it had the brand name Red October; the current inscription over the lacquer, though, said J. Becker—a Russian piano brand with a German name that didn't in fact make this instrument.

At Sergeeva's request a museum staff member pops a DVD into the television. A very old Kozin is singing:

I live in Apartment Nine
School Lane, Building One,
Where under a stern northern sun
Among the hills there grew Magadan

The song has the tenor of a patriotic love letter. There are lines about bubbling youth and a bustling wind and, of course, about love for the city in one's heart. Kozin looks frail, but his voice sounds robust.

"He is ninety years old in this recording," says Sergeeva. "But of course we overlaid a younger voice recording."

Of course.

The next song compares Magadan to Paris, which Kozin never saw—but even if he did, he sings, he would still be "in love with Magadan"—a line that rhymes with Yves Montand, whose city of Paris, Kozin asserts, couldn't possibly compare to Kozin's Magadan.

Kozin was brought to Magadan in shackles at the end of the Second World War, after more than three years of performing for Red Army soldiers on the front lines. Legend has it that he enjoyed the favor of a Gulag administrator's wife and was granted relatively lenient conditions in exchange for entertaining the camp brass. When he was released in 1952, Kozin was appointed to lead a song-and-dance troupe named for Dzerzhinsky, the founder of the secret police. The members of the troupe were all Gulag staff: Kozin became commander of the dancing camp guards.

After his release he lived in Magadan, renting rooms or parts of rooms in one communal apartment after another. In 1968, Kozin went on strike. He refused to go on tour with the local musical theater troupe if the city didn't finally provide him with a permanent place to live. He was granted a one-room apartment in this five-story building. Twenty-five years later, for Kozin's ninetieth birthday, the city gifted him the larger apartment next door—it came with the baby grand. The singer died six months later.

I ask Sergeeva how long Kozin's term of restricted-release lasted—the amount of time he was required to live in Kolyma after his release from the camp.

"I don't know." She shrugs. "He just didn't want to leave. He didn't really have anywhere to go. Here, people knew him and loved him."

In fact, people knew and loved Kozin all over the vast country—or they had, until he disappeared into the camps and listening to his music became a subversive act.

"What was his article?" I ask. This is Russian for "what was his crime"—it assumes that there was probably no crime, only an article of the criminal code that was used to process someone's transition from the outside to the inside of the Gulag.

"His articles weren't very good," says Sergeeva. She sounds uncomfortable. "His main articles that were used, they were what was then called 'man lying with man.'"

Of course, I knew the answer in advance—for Russian queers Kozin is an idol and a martyr. But I want the keeper of Kozin's memory to acknowledge it.

"When he was seventeen, he became a victim of rape," she continues. "Boys who have experienced sexual violence have a very hard time forming relationships as adults. It wasn't his fault. And he was never accused of raping children, which is the only thing that matters. Everything else is a private matter. I don't think you should be writing about this."

She slides open a wall panel, and we enter the tiny apartment next door, Kozin's actual residence for the last twenty-five years of his life. It is crammed full of furniture: a bed, a large desk, a round table for entertaining, a huge radio salvaged from a ship, and bookshelves all around.

"The bookshelves were stuffed with books two rows deep," says Sergeeva. "We've cleaned it up." They removed one row of books and all the newspapers and magazines that Kozin saved—and discarded them. There are still thirteen boxes of stuff that hasn't been catalogued, she tells me, and ten thousand letters that no one has reviewed.

The tiny kitchen contains sound-recording equipment and a two-burner electrical stove.

"He heated up food for his cats here. He had two. They were the only living beings who were always at his side."

"Did he have much of a personal life in this town?" I ask casually.

Sergeeva stares at me for a moment.

"What do you mean by a 'personal life'?"

I pretend not to understand the question.

"He didn't have a family," she says. "He did have close friends, and he corresponded with them. He never did change his psychological makeup, his situation."

"No special someone?"

"No woman in his life, and no children," Sergeeva continues. She seems to think that I am being dense. In her mind, it seems, there is no such thing that could constitute the "personal life" of a homosexual—but even the word "homosexual" is unspeakable.

"He was impotent," she says finally. "But you shouldn't write about that."

In the week after we left Magadan, everyone who had had contact with us got a visit from the FSB.

Epilogue: The Sculpture Garden

After Svetlana Boym and I visited the Sculpture Garden in 1997, I checked in on it regularly. Things changed and stayed the same. I had children, they grew old enough to attend school, and I happened to choose one just up the block from the Sculpture Garden. The kindergarten teacher took the children to the Sculpture Garden for a walk every day, so for a year in the late 2000s I entered the Sculpture Garden every weekday afternoon to see six-year-olds playing there. I could see how well the cacophony worked: If the garden had been populated only with the discards of "monumental propaganda," the park would have been a menacing, serious place; the sculptures there would have meant something. But diluted with Adam and Eve and a variety of other white plaster figures, the monuments became a neutral presence, markers of space and nothing more.

Across the street, Gorky Park was undergoing its own transformations. In the late 1990s, it acquired a number of old but serviceable Western amusement-park rides. By day, it attracted families with small children; as the sun began to set, men with beer and vodka bottles descended on the park and the families scattered. In 2011, the city undertook a major renovation of the park, turning it into hipster haven. The rides disappeared, and in came tasteful cafes, beanbag chairs and chaise longues out on the lawn, overpriced bicycle rentals, and free wifi. The grand entrance to the park, complete with three differently modified Soviet state seals and a portrait of Lenin in relief, were beautifully restored, as were various other decorations of the park. New kiosks that sold ice cream or housed the skate rental service in winter were built to look like shops from 1950s Soviet films. It was a Soviet theme park, and it was a hit with Moscow millennials.

In 2013 Moscow's flagship hipster magazine asked me to debate the city's minister of culture, Sergei Kapkov, the main architect of

154 the Gorky Park restoration project. He even invited me to meet in Gorky Park to record the discussion. I criticized the restoration—and the Sculpture Garden, which was now officially a part of Gorky Park—for creating an ahistorical space.

"You are wrong," said Kapkov. "One can't escape the historical environment. Yes, there is a lot that's Soviet and imperial about Gorky Park. And yes, unfortunately, this park was constructed during the blood-soaked decade of the 1930s. But we are compelled to live in the geometry created by the architects of that time, and we must preserve it. This is history. You are right that any public space must underscore the connection between generations. When you go to Hyde Park [in London], you know that a hundred years ago it was roughly the same: the same pond, the same footpaths. We have a different history, a more complicated one. But what are we going to do?"

I told him that the problem of what to do with the architectural legacy of state terror has been addressed elsewhere—most notably, in Berlin, where restorers have created critical distance by framing, encasing, or marking spaces to draw attention to their history. Kapkov objected that there was no single person who had the right to determine the precise critical distance required.

"Where is the guarantee that someone else isn't going to come see me tomorrow and tell me that historicity doesn't look like you are saying it does but looks completely different?"

"There is no guarantee," I said. "You'll have to assume that responsibility."

"I'm not trying to avoid responsibility," said the minister. "This is my position. I want to create a space where you and I can sit while Communist Party members sit one table over and drink tea from a samovar."

I did get one concession: Kapkov promised that he would have the placard on the Dzerzhinsky statue in the Sculpture Garden changed to reflect the fact that the monument to the founder of the secret police was removed from Lubyanka Square following the defeat of the KGB-engineered coup in 1991. Kapkov even issued instructions on changing the placard while we were sitting in Gorky Park drinking coffee.[xxii]

It's not that there is no place in Moscow where memory of the terror is preserved. The Memorial Society, though it has been declared a "foreign agent," still mounts exhibits and lectures in its space in central Moscow; the Sakharov Center is a small building not far away, and it houses a thorough permanent exhibit on political persecution; and the Gulag Museum has a sparse but expertly curated core exhibit that moved into a new building in 2016. In the attic of the Gulag Museum, in an unmarked room that few visitors know about, there is an exhibit devoted to a contest for a monument to the victims of "political repressions" to be erected in Moscow. The winning entry, by Moscow sculptor Georgy Frangulyan, is called the Wall of Sorrow. It is a section of a circle composed of stylized human figures. On a screen in the attic room, Putin, in an endless loop, repeats that "it is symbolic that the monument will be erected using not only government funding but also funds donated by the citizens." Construction of the monument commenced in the summer of 2017—but until then, it existed only in the attic of this museum. Indeed, all memorialization in Moscow lived behind closed doors. On the outside, there were restored Soviet parks—Gorky Park was followed by several others, as richly monumentally decorated—and a Metro station in the center of town, where in

2009 Stalin's name was restored as a repeated part of the decoration. It had been deleted from all the friezes where it appeared after Khrushchev's 1956 speech, but the Putin-era renovation project brought it back. In the spring of 2017, as the Moscow Metro geared up for a celebration of its eighty-second anniversary—it was launched just before the Great Terror—one of the stations was decorated with a giant portrait of Stalin and a red banner welcoming Stalin to the station; it was apparently a replica of the banner that had been draped here eighty-two years earlier. There has also been repeated talk of returning Dzerzhinsky to his place of honor in the center of town—it hasn't happened, but the space stays vacant. Human rights activists had hoped that a monument to victims of the terror would some day stand there, but the government picked a different location.

In the summer of 2016, I went to check on the Sculpture Garden again. Things had changed, and they had stayed the same. The Dzerzhinsky placard had not been changed, Kapkov's promise notwithstanding. But the sculptures had been moved around. Some appeared to have been arranged in a composition. The stones-in-a-cage monument to victims of terror—the one Sergeeva dreams of erecting in Magadan—stood in a small clearing. Its placard identified it in Russian as a "monument to the victims of the totalitarian regime," but the English translation on the same placard rendered the last word in the plural: "regimes." To its right was the Soviet state seal with the words "USSR is a stronghold of peace." A statue of Yakov Sverdlov, the first head of the Bolshevik government (until his death in 1919, at the age of thirty-three), towered over the monument to the victims of the regime. A pensive Stalin stood in

front of the monument to the victims, partially obscuring the view. Across the walkway, a tiny, skinny Andrei Sakharov sat looking up at the sky.

Did someone work to make it look like the late dissident was asking the heavens to bear witness to this travesty of memory? Or was I simply conjuring meaning out of the cacophony of stone figures all around me? There were dozens, and I could not identify most of them or see a reason for them to be—or not to be—in this park. Without a doubt, that is how most visitors to the Sculpture Garden felt about all the monuments here.

Robert Conquest, *The Great Terror: A Reassessment* (2008). This is the fortieth-anniversary edition of the book that began the Western conversation about the Gulag. When the British historian published his original work, titled *The Great Terror: Stalin's Purge of the Thirties,* he had only the very limited information released by Nikita Khrushchev's government to work with. Still, Conquest argued that the roots of terror lay not so much with Stalin personally but in the very nature of the regime. This position was much criticized by Western Sovietologists at the time, but documents released in the late 1980s proved Conquest prescient in his interpretation of history. This occasioned an updated edition of *The Great Terror,* published in 1990—to which the latest version of the book is essentially similar.

Alexander Solzhenitsyn, *The Gulag Archipelago.* Numerous editions of this book have become available since its first publication in an English translation in 1973. For most readers, an abridged edition should be enough to understand the immensity of the undertaking and the enormity of the phenomenon. The full work comprises seven books, most often packaged in three volumes. Solzhenitsyn called this book an "experiment in literary investigation." There is no narrator, omniscient or otherwise: The work is a polyphony of stories based on over two hundred interviews with former inmates. As a cross between an oral history and a novel, it is a precursor of sorts to the work of Svetlana Alexievich, the 2015 Nobel laureate. A former Gulag inmate himself, Solzhenitsyn worked on this book in secret for a decade, completing it in 1968. Unable to publish it in the Soviet Union, he smuggled the manuscript out of the country. The first volume of the *Archipelago* was published in Russian in Paris in 1973. The following year, Solzhenitsyn—who had been awarded the Nobel Prize for literature before his magnum opus was published—was exiled from the Soviet Union. It would be another sixteen years before the *Archipelago* could be published in the USSR, and another four before Solzhenitsyn returned to live in Russia.

Varlam Shalamov, *Kolyma Tales* (1995, translated by John Glad) or *Kolyma Stories* (2018, translated by Donald Rayfield). (These are two different translations of the same book). Shalamov was in many ways the opposite of Solzhenitsyn. He had no use for the heroic or the political. He set out to document not the superhuman scale of the Gulag but the miserable insignificance of the inmate. He produced a thousand of the most harrowing and claustrophobic pages in the history of literature. Like Solzhenitsyn's, his work could not be published in the Soviet Union. Unlike Solzhenitsyn,

Shalamov didn't live to see his words in print in Russia. He died in 1982, at the age of 75, deaf and nearly blind and confined to a psychiatric ward.

Anne Applebaum, *Gulag: A History* (2003). The definitive history of the Gulag was written half a century after Stalin's death—by an American journalist. Applebaum traces the roots of the Gulag, documents the numbers of inmates and casualties, and debunks the popular myth that the Gulag constituted an efficient economy. She received the Pulitzer Prize for the book in 2004.

Ingrid Carlberg, *Raoul Wallenberg: The Heroic Life and Mysterious Disappearance of the Man Who Saved Thousands of Hungarian Jews From Disappearance* (2016). By the time Swedish journalist Carlberg set out to write her version of the story, it was widely believed that there was nothing new to be learned or said about Wallenberg. Carlberg proved the skeptics wrong by providing a fundamental new account.

Alexander Etkind, *Warped Mourning: Stories of the Undead in the Land of the Unburied* (2013) and Alexander Etkind, Rory Finnin, et al, *Remembering Katyn* (2012). Cultural historian Alexander Etkind, educated as a psychologist in St. Petersburg and a philosopher in Helsinki, is one of the world's most original thinkers on Russia's past and present. Between 2010 and 2014, Etkind ran a €1 million study of "memory wars in Eastern Europe"at the University of Cambridge. Two of the books that came out of that project examine the difficulties—not to say the impossibility—of memory work in post-Soviet Russia.

Catherine Merridale, *Night of Stone: Death and Memory in Twentieth-Century Russia* (2002); Svetlana Boym, *The Future of Nostalgia* (2002); Milan Kundera, *The Book of Laughter and Forgetting* (1999). These are three very different books —the first by a historian, the second by a literary scholar, and the third a work of fiction—but all three are mentioned in this text and all three were important in shaping my understanding of memory. Merridale's is a deep dive, worth it for the stunning introduction alone. Boym's is a spectacularly erudite journey through the memory-scapes of four post-totalitarian cities. And Kundera just delightfully throws everything into question.

NOTES

i   Hanna Arendt, *The Origins of Totalitarianism* (New York: Harcourt Brace Jovanovich, 1973), p. 452.

ii   Milan Kundera, *The Book of Laughter and Forgetting* (New York: Harper Perennial, 1999), pp. 20–21.

iii   Masha Gessen, "Posledniy etap," *Itogi*, Issue 44, 1997, reproduced in *Stengazeta*, 15 March 2007, http://stengazeta.net/?p=10002981 Accessed December 16, 2016.

iv   "Rech Khrushcheva na XX s'yezde Partii," http://www.coldwar.ru/hrushev/cult_of_personality.php Accessed December 16, 2016.

v   Yevgeniy Lukin, *Nu pulachakh krovi net. Tipy i nravy Leningradskogo NKVD* (St. Petersburg: Bibliopolis, 1996).

vi   Interview with Irina Flige, in person, St. Petersburg, April 2016; Alexander Cherkasov, "Sovershivshiye nevozmozhnoye," Memorial, http://hro.org/node/305 Accessed December 18, 2016; Alexander Cherkasov, "Preuspevshiy v nevozmozhnom," Memorial, http://hro.org/node/123 Accessed December 18, 2016; Anatoly Razumov, "Skorbniy put'. Solovetskiye etapy 1937–1938 gg.," http://www.bcloedelo.ru/researches/article/?369 Accessed December 18, 2016.

vii   Interview with Veniamin Iofe, in person, Medvezhya Gora, October 27, 1997.

viii   Interview with Yuri Dmitriev, in person, Medvezhya Gora, October 27, 1997.

ix   Alexander Etkind, *Warped Mourning: Stories of the Undead in the Land of the Unburied* (Stanford University Press, 2013), p. 173.

x   Etkind, p. 172.

xi   Etkind, p. 174.

xii   Catherine Merridale, *Night of Stone: Death and Memory in Twentieth-Century Russia* (Viking, 2000), pp. 5–6.

xiii   Veniamin Iofe, *Granitsy smysla* (Memorial, 2002).

xiv   Iosilevich (Ioselevich) Aleksandr Solomonovich, "Virtual'niy muzey Gulaga," http://gulagmuseum.org/showObject.do?object=1664933&language=1 Accessed January 7, 2017.

xv   Etkind, p. 88.

xvi   M. Jacobson, M.B. Smirnov, "Sistema mest zaklyucheniya v RSFSR I SSSR. 1917–1930," in *Sistema ispravitel'no-trudovykh lagerey v SSSR*, N.G. Okhotin, A.B. Roginsky, eds (Moscow: Zvenya, 1998) http://www.memo.ru/history/nkvd/gulag/index.htm Accessed February 6, 2017.

xvii   M. B. Smirnov, S. P. Sigachev, D. V. Shkapov, "Sistema mest zaklyucheniya v RSFSR I SSSR. 1929–1960," in *Sistema ispravitel'no-trudovykh lagerey v SSSR*, *N.G. Okhotin, A.B. Roginsky*, eds (Moscow: Zvenya, 1998) http://www.memo.ru/history/nkvd/gulag/index.htm Accessed February 6, 2017; Document #100, "Spravki 1 spetsotdela MVD SSSR o kolichestve arestovannykh I osuzhdyonnykh v period 1921–1953 gg.," published by the Alexander N. Yakovlev Foundation, http://www.alexanderyakovlev.org/fond/issues-doc/1009312 Accessed February 6, 2017; Victor Zemskov, "GULAG (Istoriko-sotsiologicheskiy aspekt)," Sotsiologicheskiye issledovaniya ##6, 7, 1991, archived at http://scepsis.net/library/id_937.html Accessed February 6, 2017.

xviii   "Pis'ma I zayavleniya zaklyuchennykh," *Khroniki tekushchikh sobytiy*, 1977, reproduced at http://www.memo.ru/history/DISS/chr/XTC45_21.htm, accessed February 4, 2017.

xix   Varlam Shalamov, "Sukhim paykom," http://shalamov.ru/library/2/9.html Accessed February 8, 2017. My translation.

xx   Dmitry Minchonok, "Kak nam bylo strashno!" *Ogonyok*, March 3, 2002, http://www.kommersant.ru/doc/2289979. Accessed February 18, 2017.

xxi   "Memorial 'Maska skorbi' Ernsta Neizvestnogo khotyat ustanovit' v Yekatirenburge," unsigned news item, gazeta.ru, August 10, 2016, https://www.gazeta.ru/culture/news/2016/08/10/n_8979329.shtml Accessed February 15, 2017.

xxii   "Sergei Kapkov I Masha Gessen sporyat o sotrudnichestve s gosudarstvom," *Afisha*, July 26, 2013, https://daily.afisha.ru/archive/gorod/archive/kapkov-vs-gessen/ Accessed February 20, 2017.

Cover: Ust'-Omchug, Kolyma

Page 8: Bust of Wallenberg, Library of Foreign Literature courtyard, Moscow

Pages 18–19: Site of mass executions, Kovalevsky forest, St. Petersburg. The Kremlin once promised Memorial Society that a museum of terror would be constructed at this site. Plans were drafted and submitted to then president Dmitry Medvedev. But final approval never came.

Pages 20–21: A model of a monument to victims of totalitarian terror, Sculpture Garden, Gorky Park, Moscow

Pages 22–23: Perm-36

Pages 24–25: Sandarmokh

Pages 26–27: Execution order signed by all members of the Politburo, including Stalin, State Museum of Gulag History, Moscow

Page 28: Butugychag

Page 29: Perm–36

Pages 30–31: The harbor of Magadan

Pages 32–33, 34: Butugychag

Pages 35: Mask of Sorrow, Magadan

Pages 36–37: The last remaining Gulag structure in Ust'-Omchug, long used as an office by geologists, now stands unidentifiable

Page 38–39: A photo of poet Evgenia Mustangova (a pseudonym that referred to her mane of hair), killed in Sandarmokh, was made into a small memorial plaque at the site; it has been repeatedly vandalized

Page 40: Burial map, Sandarmokh (fragment)

Page 61: NKVD mugshot, Memorial archives, Saint Petersburg

Pages 62–63: Perm-36

Page 64: Kovalevsky Forest

Pages 65, 66–67: Perm-36

Pages 68–69: Perm

Page 70: Elizaveta Delibash's family album, with no photos

Page 71: The sole surviving image of Nina Delibash

Pages 72–73: Perm-36

Pages 74–75: The harbor of Magadan

Pages 76–77: A vent in the ceiling of the uranium-processing plant in Butugychag

Pages 78–79, 80–81: Stalin, Lenin, the Soviet state seal, and the slogan THE USSR IS THE BULWARK OF PEACE, Sculpture Garden, Moscow

Pages 82–83: Metal window shutters from the ruins of a Gulag-era jail, outskirts of Magadan

Page 84: Mug shot, Memorial archives, St. Petersburg

Page 85: A memorial sign, Sandarmokh (fragment)

Pages 86–87: The central square of Medvezhyegorsk, capital of the White Sea Canal construction project; before execution, the victims of Sandarkmokh were held in a barracks here

Page 88: Nina Delibash

Page 89: Complete works of Lenin, library of Perm-36

Pages 90–91: Elizaveta Delibash, St. Petersburg

Page 92: Furnace, uranium processing plant, Butugychag

Page 109: NKVD mug shot, Memorial archives, St. Petersburg

Page 110–111: Perm-36

Pages 112–113: A trinity of revered Russians on a poster outside the Railway Transport College in central Moscow: Czar Nicholas II, Soviet secret police founder Felix Dzerzhinsky, and Stalin

Pages 114–115: Putin, Stalin, and Lenin impersonators, Red Square, Moscow

Pages 116–117: House of Culture, Medvezhyegorsk

Pages 118–119: Medvezhyegorsk

Pages 120–121: World War II memorial, Medvezhyegorsk

Page 122: NKVD mug shot, Memorial archives, St. Petersburg (fragment)

Pages 123, 124–125: Marker on the grave of a Gulag guard, Butugychag

Pages 126–127: Magadan

Pages 128–129: Statue of Sergei Kirov, White Sea Canal headquarters, Medvezhyegorsk

Pages 130–131: White Sea Canal headquarters, Medvezhyegorsk

Pages 132–133: Remains of a Gulag jail, Magadan

Pages 134–135; 136–137: Butugychag

Page 138: Names written on wooden markers, Sandarmokh

Columbia Global Reports is a publishing imprint from Columbia University that commissions authors to do original on-site reporting around the globe on a wide range of issues. The resulting novella-length books offer new ways to look at and understand the world that can be read in a few hours. Most readers are curious and busy. Our books are for them.

Subscribe to Columbia Global Reports and get six books a year in the mail in advance of publication.
globalreports.columbia.edu/subscribe

2017

The Global Novel:
Writing the World in the
21st Century
Adam Kirsch

Another Fine Mess:
America, Uganda, and the
War on Terror
Helen C. Epstein

Nollywood:
The Making of a Film Empire
Emily Witt

2018

Pipe Dreams:
The Plundering of Iraq's
Oil Wealth
Erin Banco

Never Remember:
Searching for Stalin's Gulags
in Putin's Russia
Masha Gessen and Misha
Friedman

High-Speed Empire:
Chinese Expansion and the
Future of Southeast Asia
Will Doig